Model Rocketry

HOBBY OF TOMORROW

Launching of a large single-stage model rocket.

PETER LOWRY
FIELD GRIFFITH

Model Rocketry
HOBBY OF TOMORROW

DRAWINGS BY RITCHIE LOWRY

DOUBLEDAY & COMPANY, INC.

GARDEN CITY, NEW YORK

To our parents and sisters

ISBN: 0-385-03076-2 TRADE
0-385-05236-7 PREBOUND
Library of Congress Catalog Card Number 74-143815

9 8 7 6 5 4 3 2

Contents

Preface

We first thought of writing this book the summer we were thirteen. Although we had read everything we could find on model rocketry, we were frustrated by the fact that the material was either too technical or too elementary. Furthermore, it was scattered through a wide variety of newsletters, magazines, technical reports, and books. By personal experience we were learning daily not only what to do but what not to do. We thought we could spare other model rocketeers a lot of stupid mistakes.

By the time we were fifteen we were convinced a book was the thing. We found we had learned most of the answers to the questions we had when we started, looked up the rest, and set about putting them into a form recognizable by other kids. Now we are seventeen and here it is.

We want to say thanks to all the people who have read and commented on the manuscript and especially to our editors who believed from the start that being young was not a handicap. Also to classmates Dave Moon and Don Larson and the many model rocketeers who shared the agonies with us.

PETER LOWRY Wayland, Massachusetts
FIELD GRIFFITH Washington, D.C.

CHAPTER 1

Why kill yourself?

What can go off like a hand grenade, start six fires in the dead leaves, could blow your hand off, requires bunkers like Cape Kennedy's, and soars to an altitude of two feet?

Answer: a match-head rocket. And we were the idiots behind it. The really stupid thing is we could have been sending rockets up 2000 feet, learning something about real scientific research, and enjoying the flights instead of dodging shrapnel and smothering fires.

We figured that as long as it wasn't a home-brewed propellant coming out of our chemistry labs we didn't qualify as "basement bombers," but we were just that dumb and came just that close to being statistics. The American Rocket Society estimates that an amateur working with his own engines and propellants has a one-in-seven chance of being maimed or killed for each year he continues his experimentation. Between us, we'd been fooling around for six years, and *that's* really pushing it.

Our own version of suicide consisted of half a pound of match heads crammed into a container. We found out later that three match heads can drive a hollow metal bolt with the force of a bullet. We didn't know then about model rocketry, one of the safest hobbies known (an injury of any consequence has yet to be reported).

The model rocketeer flies lightweight, non-metallic, re-coverable, and reflyable rockets using commercially produced rocket engines that do not require the handling, loading, or compounding of explosive materials by the user. This is better than being a "basement bomber" and, most important, much much safer.

Look at it this way: model rockets, like model airplanes, are made of balsa, paper, plastic, and other non-metallic materials. A model rocket has a built-in recovery system to return it to the ground safely so it may be flown again and again. It is launched electrically by remote control and guided in flight by fins, tail rings, or other devices.

The science of model rocketry involves many things, all worth knowing and all quite interesting. Consider optics, aerodynamics, mathematics, electronics, mechanics, engineering, dynamics, medicine, astronomy, and meteorology, to name a few.

You build model rockets with the same tools you've used for other models: airplane glue, transparent tape, dope, balsa, and paper. Many companies make rocket kits you can assemble in less than twenty minutes. Some kits cost less than a dollar. Why kill yourself?

Except at the nozzle, model rocket engines generate very little heat when ignited. That's why you can use paper and balsa. If metal were used, you would not only have a potential hazard but the weight would be a real problem. (Some steel weighs ¼ pound per cubic inch.)

A metal rocket that changes direction in flight and hits an object or a living thing can cause severe damage and might even kill. A rocket made of paper and balsa absorbs the shock. Your model rocket is safe enough to be used without bunkers and requires no technical assistance to build, and you can launch and recover it in an area the size of a football field.

Model rockets have been officially endorsed by the Air Force and duplicate nearly everything done at White Sands, New Mexico, and Cape Kennedy, Florida. The language

Exhibit of United States model rocketry at the Smithsonian Institution, Washington, D.C.

of model rocketry is the same as that used by the professionals. "Specific impulse," "N-seconds," "thrust," "exhaust velocity," and "static testing" mean the same to model and professional rocketeers alike.

You'll find there is often a confusion between *amateur* and *model* rocketry. This confusion has resulted in unnecessary laws and regulations. Amateur rocketry involves the compounding of explosives by the user and the making of rockets out of metal. When supervised by men trained in the handling of explosives and internal ballistics, it is a relatively safe but serious business. Model rocketry, on the other hand, is a safe hobby which gives you the same result and a chance to experiment without the danger.

In California, model rocketry was once specifically outlawed along with amateur rocketry. Finally someone made the distinction and the law was changed to permit model rocketry but still restrain amateur rocketry. Not all states have been this progressive. In Massachusetts, the same law that stopped Robert Hutchings Goddard in 1926 was in effect until late 1969 and was used to curtail model rocketry in that state.

The Federal Aviation Administration (FAA) has stringent regulations covering amateur and professional rocketry, especially regarding use of the air lanes. Model rocketry, however, doesn't fall in either of these categories and is a safe substitute for both.

A survey conducted in early 1962 showed only two of 1379 returned questionnaires with reports of accidents involving model rocketry. One rocketeer burned his finger on Nichrome igniter wire and another broke his arm trying to retrieve a model rocket from a tree. In contrast, 218 reported accidents involving "basement bombers," and these cited accidents that killed, crippled, or maimed.[1]

Not only have hundreds of unsupervised amateurs been killed in "basement bomber" activities, but accidents have also happened when supervised by responsible (but unqualified) adults. For example, in Floydada, Texas, a rocket made from a piece of pipe exploded in a high school chemistry class, killing the teacher and injuring seven students. The teacher was a former employee of the Atomic Energy Commission Research Center at Los Alamos, New Mexico, but he was not qualified to build a rocket. Neither are we and neither are you.

Model rocketry is a hobby that had to happen when the Space Age began. Before 1958 and the launching of Sputnik, young people were satisfied with model airplanes, but

[1] Statistics from "A Rocketeer's Guide to Avoid Suicide," Estes Industries, 1964.

A model rocket launching at a National Association of Rocketry-sanctioned meet in Virginia.

from then on rocket power and jet propulsion became the thing. Fortunately for all of us, it was about that time the safe commercial model rocket engine came out.

Rockets themselves have a history going back to solid-fuel skyrockets built by the Chinese in the thirteenth century. In the 1800s, solid-fuel rockets were used as weapons until more powerful and accurate artillery was developed. The liquid-fuel rocket, developed by America's Robert Goddard, was used extensively as a weapon by the Germans during World War II. (The U. S. Government had little interest in rocketry—then.)

Model rocketry was begun by the men who were involved in professional rocketry and who wanted a more manageable way to test their theories. It didn't start with hobby stores and toys, so a lot of kids didn't find out about it right away. Fortunately, it's growing in popularity, though rocket supplies still are purchased mainly through mail order by model rocketeers or rocket clubs.

You'll be interested to know that being a model rocketeer puts you in the Space Race. The Soviet Union and its satellite countries have gone in for model rocketry in a big way. Poland, East Germany, Hungary, Czechoslovakia, Bulgaria, and Yugoslavia all have active clubs, and model rocketry is actually *required* in the public schools of the U.S.S.R. Clubs in these countries are government-sponsored and organized. (Russia has over 5000 state-supported clubs.[2]) Early international competitions were dominated by these countries.

At first only the United States participated on behalf of the non-Communist world, and we didn't exactly lead the field. Now other countries such as Australia, Canada, Belgium, Great Britain, and Sweden have discovered model rocketry and are coming along too.

[2] "Birth of a Vocation," Soviet Embassy, Washington, D.C.

Model rocketry photograph in the U.S.S.R. pavilion, "Man and His World" exhibit, Montreal, Canada.

CHAPTER 2

We want to say this about that

There are two types of beginners in model rocketry. One has access to the facilities of a model rocket club; the other must either purchase or make his own tools and instruments. If you already have modeling materials, you may be ready to roll. In any case, read this chapter carefully.

Regardless of the type of beginner you are, the following supplies are minimal for working with model rockets. In addition to a working space, you will need notebooks, a couple of knives, masking tape, transparent tape, sandpaper, paintbrushes, paint, sanding sealer, model airplane cement, white glue, and a model rocket kit. Later on you can think about your own designs. Start with a kit. (Kits are available at some hobby stores and by mail from the companies listed in Appendix 1.)

First of all, you must have a place to work. This could be a workbench, a section of a workbench, or even a card table covered with newspaper. It should be some place where your work can be left undisturbed (in other words, not the pool table) and out of reach of younger brothers and sisters. Don't work in a closet—your work space needs ventilation. Usually an open window will be enough.

We recommend keeping at least two notebooks: one for notes and designs and another for data sheets and technical reports. Unless you have a photographic memory, you will need to write down the results of tests and flights.

You will need a regular hobby knife, the type that can be used with an assortment of inexpensive replaceable blades, and a jackknife. The jack is used to whittle and carve balsa parts. Keep all blades sharp. In the case of the hobby knife, we think it is just as well to throw out the dull razor blade and replace it. A jackknife has to be sharpened on a whetstone, of course.

The paper-backed masking tape is helpful not only to mask for a neat paint job, but also to label boxes of parts and to hinge the wing flaps on boost-gliders.

That ½-inch-wide transparent tape is for fastening the shroud lines on parachutes, making fast repairs on models, and shimming small balsa or paper parts. "Shimming" is winding tape around a small piece so that it fits snugly inside a larger space. An engine is usually shimmed with tape so that it doesn't slip from the rocket body tube during flight.

Have a good selection of paper and Mylar-backed sandpaper on hand. The best grits for the model rocketeer are extra fine, fine, and medium. You'll only need small pieces of sandpaper in model rocketry, and even those go a long way. Sandpaper is for sanding, forming, and smoothing balsa and paper.

Obtain a set of small camel's-hair paintbrushes. Sizes ⚹1, ⚹3, and ⚹6 are best for model rocketry. The small brushes will be used for details and the large for painting the big areas.

Paint is used to show off a model as well as to aid in tracking. Beginning model rocketeers should have at least four different colors, plus paint thinner. We recommend orange, black, white, and silver so the rocket may be more easily seen during flight. These paints may be enamel or nitrate-based or butyrate-based dope (lacquer). Use enamel for plastics and dope for balsa and paper.

Liquid sanding sealer is recommended for finishing balsa parts and for sealing body tubes. It is applied with a brush and, after it has dried, the surface is sanded smooth. The more this applying-sanding cycle is repeated, the glossier the surface becomes. Sealer and paints are available in hobby shops or from the various model rocket companies.

You'll need both white glue and model airplane cement. Use white glue for joining engine blocks, anchoring shock cords, and setting screw eyes. Model airplane cement is best for general purposes. CAUTION: Do not use model airplane cement on plastic or rubber.

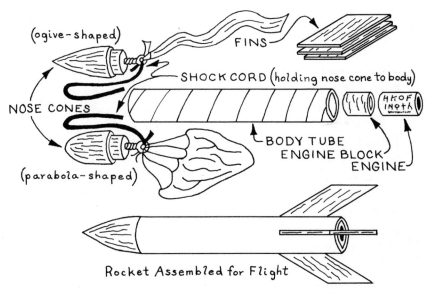

Basic parts for a simple solid-fuel model rocket using parachute or streamer recovery systems. See photo on page 15. Some details, like protective wadding, are missing from this sketch and will be discussed in later chapters.

Although not essential to the beginner, the following tools make things easier: wire cutters, scissors, soldering iron, vise, C-clamp, tweezers, pencils, and felt-tipped pens.

Let's examine the parts of a model rocket. The central component is a body tube, open at both ends. Body tubes are always non-metallic, and it is easier to buy than to make them. Most tubes are paper (though there is a light-weight Mylar body tube available) and spiral-wound—that is, two or three layers of paper with spirals going in opposite directions for strength.

If you're really dedicated to working hard for a finished product and have a design that does not adapt to the body tubes available, you can make your own. It's not easy and be prepared to scrap most of your early efforts. Technical reports and sources containing how-to-do-it information are listed in the Selected Readings.

A nose cone is fitted carefully into the top opening of the body tube. Its shape is seldom that of a true cone. More often than not it's the shape of an ogive or a parabola. Hemispheres, flat surfaces, and even spheres have been tried however.

Except in the case of certain types of recovery systems (all of which will be described later), the base of the nose cone must be sanded down to form a shoulder that will allow it to slip freely from the body tube and deploy a recovery device that has been tucked into the hollow of the tube. For best streamlining, the outside diameter of the nose cone itself should equal the outside diameter of the body tube.

Nose cones may be made from balsa, hardwood, rubber, plastic, wax, or any other non-metallic material. Even plastic scale models of space capsules and cones of paper have been tried.

Sometimes, in order to stabilize the rocket, a heavier nose cone is required. Again, *nose cones should always be non-*

metallic. If weight is needed, use a lead or brass nose cone weight (available from model rocket suppliers).

Many types of ready-made nose cones are available. Some purists make their own, but we think you'll find the commercial cones good enough.

Fins may be of various shapes and designs. They are usually cut with a hobby knife from thin sheets of balsa or plastic and should be cut so the balsa grain lies parallel to either the leading or trailing edge. This is for strength. If the fins are cut any other way, they are almost sure to break off in flight. Many model rocketeers do not believe this and have to try it both ways. Go ahead. Fins are cheap.

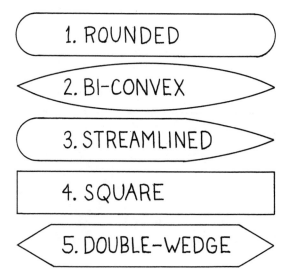

Fin airfoils.

There are five different fin airfoils (cross-section shapes) in the drawing on this page. The (3) airfoil is most efficient in reducing drag, and (4) or (5) produce high drag. The trailing edge of the fin should always be square or pointed. If it is rounded, high drag develops from the increased turbulence.

Three to six fins are usually used on model rockets. Generally, more than six fins result in high drag and fewer than three, in instability. Glue fillets are often used to cement fins on the body tube. To fillet a fin, first apply glue on the root edge. Next, cement the fin to the body tube, using the fin placement guide. After the glue has set, apply glue at the joint of the body tube and the fin. Do the same on the other side of the fin. After the glue dries, the joint will be stronger than the fin itself.

Numbers indicate placement
of fins for 3-and 4-fin rockets:

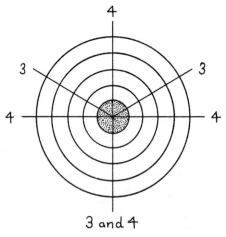

3 and 4

FIN PLACEMENT GUIDE

Sanding sealer is often used to strengthen fins and is applied, followed by sanding, just as with other balsa parts. Paper reinforcing material strengthens and smoothes fins also. At the same time, this process provides a smooth, white surface for painting.

Fins guide but do not support the rocket in flight. Therefore, a rocket must never be launched horizontally. If launched in this manner, the rocket will fall to the ground, shearing off all the fins, crumpling the body tube, and smashing the nose cone. This is disconcerting to the average model rocketeer and terrifying to his parents.

Recovery systems are necessary if a rocket is to be flown more than once. The simplest system is a "nose-blow" recovery. This simply means a system whereby the nose cone blows off the rocket and the aerodynamically unstable pieces float gently back to earth.

When a model is too heavy for nose-blow recovery, a streamer is added to slow the descent. Parachutes made of plastic, silk, nylon, or even paper are used for still heavier models.

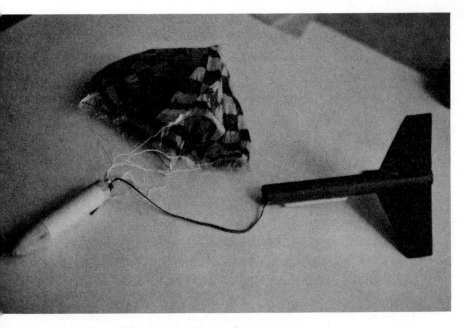

A simple model rocket with parachute recovery.

An engine block is also needed. As the rocket ascends, the thrust tends to force the engine forward into the body tube. An engine block is a balsa or paper ring which prevents this. Since it is hollow, it also allows ejection gases to blow off the nose cone and activate the recovery system. The block, too, serves to position the engine and protect the parachute or streamer.

When the nose cone is meant to blow off the model to deploy the recovery system, the engine must fit snugly in the body tube. If the engine ejects without deploying the recovery device, the rocket will streamline in and crash. A strip of masking tape wound around the casing will prevent an engine from ejecting by making it fit firmly and tightly in the body tube.

If the body tube is too big for the engine, insert a simple engine mount. This means simply installing a smaller body tube, with engine block included, in a larger body tube. This can be done with paper rings, balsa wood strips, or just plenty of masking tape.

When the engine is meant to leave the model, make sure it is free to eject. If the engine does not eject in this case, the ejection charge will blow a hole in the body tube.

Never mount an engine so the nozzle is inserted more than ¾ inch (or 20 millimeters) into the body tube or you will encounter the Krushnic Effect. This condition (named after a model rocketeer who discovered it) causes an engine to lose thrust.

Pounds, ounces, feet, inches, etc. you know. This is the English system. Model rocketry, since it is a scientific hobby, has switched to the metric system of weights and measures. Metric units are grams, newtons, liters, meters, etc. The equivalents of these to the English system are shown in Appendix 4. Metric units are easy to work with and will be used in conjunction with English units throughout.

Most model rockets are lightweight. Nearly all single-stage sport models weigh less than 1 ounce (or 30 grams) each without engine.

Well, we've just covered the basic steps of rocket construction. It will cheer you to know that even the most complex systems are only elaborations on these basics.

CHAPTER 3

Model rocket engines

The most important part of any model rocket is the engine. Over one hundred distinct types are available for just as many different uses. Before discussing these uses, however, we would like to clear up a few common misconceptions about rocket power in general.

Rockets work on the principle that *every action has an equal and opposite reaction.* Translation: if you blow up a balloon and release the neck it will skitter all around in the air. The *action* is the air being expelled; the *reaction* is the progress of the balloon. This is an example of Sir Isaac Newton's Third Law of Motion.

A lot of people think the exhaust from the rocket pushes against the launch pad and thereby lifts the rocket into the air. A rocket is not fired like a slingshot and no launch pad is needed to produce lift. You probably noticed that your balloon took off in midair. Anyway, don't feel bad if you didn't know this—a survey during the first manned space flights showed more than half of NASA's non-technical personnel didn't know Newton's Third Law either.

Model rockets are true rockets. That is, they don't require air in order to operate.

"I thought everything needed some kind of gas like oxygen in order to burn," you say.

True, but all combustible rocket propellants have an

oxidizer included in their formula. An *oxidizer* is a substance that releases a gas that supports combustion (not necessarily oxygen) when heated, burned, or brought in contact with another substance. This means the rocket carries its own gas supply. When fuel and the oxidizer are ignited together a controlled explosion takes place. This produces large volumes of gases that rush out the nozzle just as the air did in your balloon.

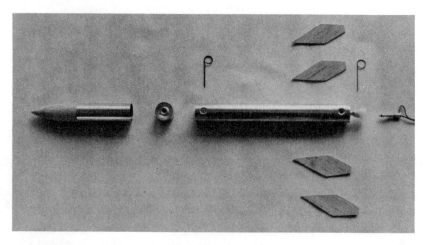

Breakdown of a liquid-fuel model rocket.

Propellants are divided into two main groups: liquid fuel and solid fuel. These are subdivided into combustible and non-combustible. "Combustible" simply means the propellant burns in order to produce thrust.

Thrust is the force that pushes the rocket through the air. Thrust is measured in *newtons*, the metric unit of force, with 4.45 newtons equal to 1 pound of thrust. Most model rocket companies have switched to the metric system and newtons, but some may stick with the English system of pounds.

Thrust is not as important as most model rocketeers think. Four newtons of constant thrust for 1.2 seconds will put a rocket up much much higher than 6 newtons for .2 seconds. For this reason model rocket engines are classified not by thrust but by *total impulse*. This is measured in *newton-seconds* (or *pound-seconds*). An engine with twice the total impulse of another engine will power a rocket to a theoretical drag-free altitude twice that of the lower impulse engine. Total impulse is equal to the average thrust multiplied by the duration.

We don't mean thrust isn't important at all. One-tenth of a newton with a duration of 100 seconds and 10 newtons of thrust with a duration of 1 second have the same total impulse, but the latter is the only engine that could be used in a model rocket. The first engine would lack the thrust to lift a model rocket, let alone get it to stabilizing velocity. For this reason, Jetex-type engines with long durations and low thrust can never be used in model rockets even though their total impulse is often equal to many standard model rocket engines.

Average thrust is the total impulse of an engine divided by the duration. Therefore, if the total impulse of an engine is 10 newton-seconds and the duration is 2 seconds, the average thrust is 5 newtons.

Duration is the time from ignition to burnout, the time the engine produces thrust.

Burnout takes place when the engine ceases to produce thrust, that is, when the propellant is used up.

Maximum thrust is the highest thrust generated by an engine. On a thrust-time curve it is represented by the highest point.

T-max is the length of time from ignition to the point of maximum thrust. In the smaller engines, this is important because a burst of high thrust is needed at the beginning of flight to stabilize your rocket.

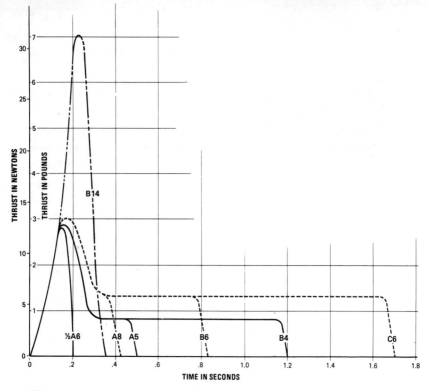

Thrust-time performance graphs for seven types of engines (see engine classifications on page 24).

A *thrust-time curve* (or *thrust-time performance graph*) is a chart of engine performance.

These are all terms from professional rocketry. In model rocketry they are used on a smaller scale, of course, but terms are terms whether the engine is 70 millimeters or 500 meters long.

Now, we know you're still nervous. Those magazine articles that say a model rocket engine is no larger than a firecracker or a shotgun shell do not really do much for the safety image. In actual fact, though, model rocket engines are safer than snowballs.

In March 1967 Estes Industries in Penrose, Colorado, released the results of tests on standard rocket engines. These engines were really put through it, and the results are tabulated in the accompanying table.

Test results of Estes Industries' attempts to cause ignition or explosion in 1/4A–C model rocket engines "accidentally

TEST	REACTIONS OF PROPELLANT	
	IGNITION	EXPLOSION
1. Run over by a 4000 lb+ Pontiac (same engine ignited later electrically)	No ---	No No
2. Penetrated by rifle bullet fired from a .303 Savage	No	No
3. Cut in half with a high-speed band saw	No	No
4. Hit two times successively with a five-pound weight dropped 20 feet		
a. Hit engine vertically	No	No
b. Hit engine horizontally	No	No
5. Subjected to an acetylene torch (cut in half a ⅛-inch steel plate nearby)	No	No
6. Soaked in gasoline and the gasoline ignited	No	No
7. The end of the engine casing suspended over a candle flame for 10 seconds (NOTE: Propellant was ¼ inch from flame)		
a. Suspended vertically	No	No
b. Suspended horizontally	No	No
8. Nozzle of an engine suspended vertically over a candle flame for 30 seconds, giving ample time for the flame to shoot up the nozzle, if it could	No	No
9. Wrapped in newspaper and the newspaper ignited	No	No
10. A burning cigarette snuffed out against the propellant grain of a booster engine	No	No
11. A tube with three engines electrically ignited in a box with thirty-three other prepackaged engines	No	No
12. A sustained fire of balsa blocks	Yes	No

NOTE: *Never* subject an engine to any of these conditions. These tests were done under *controlled* experimental conditions. Even though these tests are valid, something might go wrong. Don't you take the chance of being injured!

SOURCE: Vernon Estes, *Youth Rocket Safety* (A Report to the Model Rocket Manufacturers Association). Estes Industries, 1967, pp. 28–33.

As you can see, it is almost impossible to ignite a model rocket engine accidentally. It *is* impossible for an engine to explode accidentally. During manufacture, all engines are subjected to pressures of well over 10,000 pounds per square inch.[1]

"Well," you say, "I know the terms and I know how safe they are, but what is a *model rocket engine?!*"

We sympathize with your position.

Model rocket engines are, for the most part, small, compact, powerful, and lightweight. They contain combustible solid fuel. Except for the propellant, engines are made only of a paper casing with a ceramic nozzle. Therefore, there is little chance of injury in case it explodes.

An exception to the rule of non-metallic parts in a model rocket would be metallic liquid-fuel engines. These engines are entirely different: large, bulky, not as much power per ounce of propellant, and heavy. Instead of paper and clay, the engine is made of aluminum. This sounds unsafe, but the propellant is liquid and *non-combustible*. The casing is also light in weight so if the recovery system failed, no one would be hurt by your falling rocket.

NAR-Type Classification System

Type	Total Impulse (newton-seconds)	Total Impulse (pound-seconds)
1/4A	0.00-0.625	0.00-0.14
1/2A	0.626-1.25	0.15-0.28
A	1.26-2.50	0.29-0.56
B	2.51-5.00	0.57-1.12
C	5.01-10.00	1.13-2.24
D	10.01-20.00	2.25-4.48
E	20.01-40.00	4.49-8.96
F	40.01-80.00	8.97-17.92

Most engines are coded according to National Association of Rocketry (NAR) classification system. Take the following engine:

[1] Vernon Estes, *Youth Rocket Safety*, p. 32.

B14–6

"B" indicates the total impulse. "14" is the average thrust. In most cases this is expressed in newtons; however, since some manufacturers still use pounds, check this out. "6" is the time delay in seconds. Each single- and upper-stage model rocket engine has a delay and ejection charge. Once the actual thrust of the engine stops, your rocket is moving at a pretty good clip, usually better than 400 feet per second. A delay allows the rocket to coast to a higher altitude. Smoke is created during the delay to aid in tracking. The

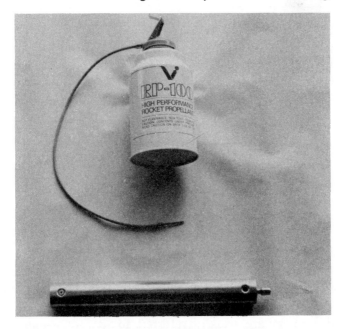

Liquid-fuel model rocket engine and fuel.

purpose of the ejection charge is to deploy the recovery device.

Some engines are followed with "0," such as B14–0, A6–0, or 1/4A3–0. In this case there is no delay or ejection

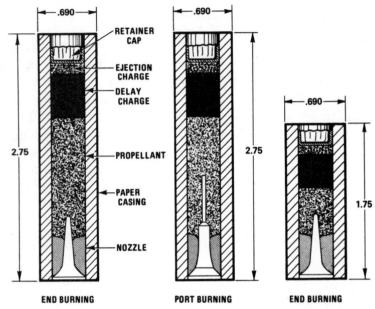

Single- and upper-stage engines (left) and booster engines (right).

charge. These engines are used primarily in the lower stages of multistage rockets. For this reason they are called *booster engines.*

There are two basic types of engines, port and end burners. Port burners, also called "core burners," have a hole drilled through the propellant grain. With more area of the propellant exposed, the engine burns faster, producing higher thrust. Because of the short burn time, the thrust-time curve for these engines indicates a rapid rise in thrust falling to zero soon after T-max.

End burners are usually referred to as "series-one engines," port burners as "series-two." A short end burner is referred to as "series-three."

The liquid-fuel engine is completely different. As shown in the photo on page 25, the fuel comes in a pressurized tank. This is dextrodichloromethane, a non-flammable, non-

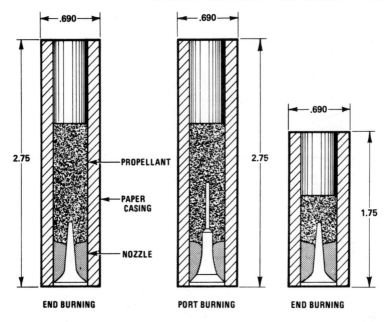

poisonous refrigerant. Under pressure it's a liquid, but when
released to normal temperature and pressure, it immediately
turns to gas. Just before launch the engine is filled with
this fuel, still under pressure. When a valve is released at
launch, by electrical or mechanical means, the gases roar
out the nozzle, producing thrust. While the propellant
has to be replaced, the metal engines may be used again
and again.

The device to deploy the recovery system is not an
explosive charge but a pneumatic air release. All this means
is that when the pressure of the gas, which forces metal
clamps to hold the recovery tube and payload section,
is gone, the clamps release the tube and the recovery device.
The placing of paper discs in a unit called the *separator*
causes the pressure to leak out slowly and therefore a delay
is introduced. The more discs, the longer the delay.

One of the great advances in model rocket engine tech-

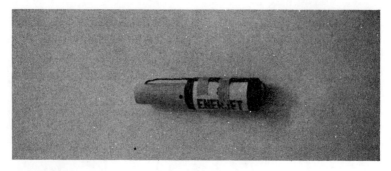

NAR Class E engine with variable time delay.

nology is the development of the variable time delay for solid-fuel rockets. This is simply a fuse connected to a separate ejection charge unit. If the fuse burns at the rate of 1 inch every 2 seconds and a 10-second delay is needed, use only 6 inches of fuse. Since the fuse is ignited in the exhaust, the thrust duration of the engine must be taken into account. This variable delay device was developed by Rocket Development Corporation for large Class D, E, and F type engines.

Another delay-ejection charge package that is being worked on now is a unit the same diameter as an engine but just including the delay and ejection charge. These units would fit almost any small 1/4A through C type engine and would be made with various delays. The procedure for their use would be to select the one needed and glue on a booster engine.

The advantages of variable delay are numerous. You have complete control over the coasting flight of your rocket. You never run out of booster engines. You don't have to buy a great number of engines with various delays. Instead, a set of booster engines and a couple of delay-ejection charge units will be sufficient.

With more than a hundred different engines available, you're sure to find the right one for the right job.

CHAPTER 4

Out to launch

It's time to separate the rocketeers from the artists. Your beautiful slick-finish three-fin job with the B14–6 engine in it won't be much more than a good paperweight if it's never launched.

Electric launching systems are the most common type. The best thing about them is that you can stay a safe distance from the launch pad and ignite the engine of your rocket by remote control. The basis for this launch system is a thin piece of Nichrome wire that glows red hot when an electric current passes through it. This is the *igniter*. Heavier wire, of course, is used between the igniter and the firing switch. The principle is the same as that of the electric light bulb.

The other type of launch system is the one used commonly in igniting fireworks—the fuse. The advantage of the fuse is that heavy and complicated electronic equipment is not needed. The disadvantages are serious, however. For one thing, fuses are not reliable, and, as it burns at a faster rate, you may have a rocket launch right into your face unless an extremely long fuse is used. Another problem is that if something happens to your rocket in the last few seconds (such as a launch rod's tipping over), there is nothing you can do to stop ignition of the rocket. One final disadvantage is that your rockets are now considered fireworks by the NAR and even by fire codes that specifically exempt model rocketry, so you may break the law unintentionally. Because of these factors, fuses won't be discussed further in this book.

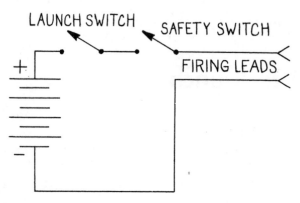

A simple electric launch system wiring (schematic).

A simple electric launch system consists of two 12-foot pieces of lamp-cord wire, a firing button, a battery, and an igniter. This, too, has its dangers—your little brother could sit on the firing button while you're hooking up the rocket, so an extra toggle switch is also needed. This is kept permanently off until the moment your rocket is ready to be launched. It's commonly referred to as a *safety switch*.

Since the model rocket has fins and not a complex gyroscope system, it needs to be guided for its first few feet of flight. Otherwise, slight irregularities in thrust or a minute breath of wind could knock it way off course. A *launch rod* or *launch tower* is the answer. A launch rod is used most often. Usually this is ⅛-inch piano wire 1 yard (or 1 meter) long. The model rocket has a small section of soda straw glued on it, which is called a *launch lug*. This slips over the launch rod and guides the rocket during launch.

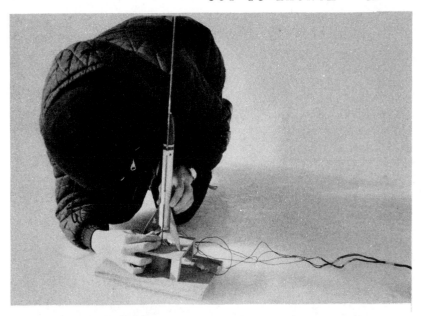

Model rocketeer David Moon attaching micro-clips (see page 39) to the igniter of small single-stage model rocket. Note that a launch rod is used in this launch system.

There are many different types of launch towers. Essentially, they all guide the fins of the rocket. For instance, one kind is simply three pieces of wood bolted to a launch pad in such a way that a three-fin model rocket will slip between the pieces of wood. Launch towers are much more rigid than launch rods and therefore can be built much taller. This improves the stability of the model rocket even more. Also, a launch lug will cause some friction and lower the altitude of the rocket. No launch lug is needed with a tower.

A recent development is the *launch rail*. This uses a lug but is much stiffer than a launch rod and is a compromise between the tower and the rod. The launch rail

One type of launch tower. Note strip-metal blast deflector.

is a tube of metal with a slot down the side. A T-shaped lug on the rocket fits into the slot. Lugs are made of thin hardwood or small nylon screws (see page 34).

CAUTION: A simple trough fireworks launcher is not safe and should never be used to launch model rockets.

A model rocket being launched from a tower.

A model rocket should never be launched more than 30 degrees from the vertical. A model rocket's fins do not give any lift at all—their purpose is to stabilize the rocket in flight. A model rocket launched anywhere near horizontal will, because of gravity, simply fall and skitter

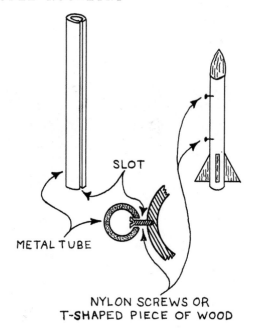

SLOT

METAL TUBE

NYLON SCREWS OR
T-SHAPED PIECE OF WOOD

A launch rail system.

on the ground, a substantial danger to spectators.

There is always the possibility of irregularities in model rocket engines. If an excessive angle from the vertical is used and the engine stalled for a second, the rocket might change course and dive earthward under full power. And, believe us, a model rocket moving at 600 miles per hour is no joke to anyone underneath. The impact also does wonders for your rocket!

Every launch pad should be protected by a *blast deflector*. This serves a dual purpose: (a) protecting the launch pad from burning and (b) deflecting flame away from your model rocket's fins. Deflectors may be made of a thin sheet of any metal except aluminum or magnesium. A deflector is shown in the photo on page 32.

Now for igniters. There are two kinds of igniters for solid-fuel rockets. One is based on Nichrome wire and the other on a hair-trigger mechanism. There is also a special type for liquid-fuel rockets.

Nichrome wire was the first type of ignition ever to be used in model rocketry and still is the most common. It is used alone or in combination with other ignitable materials.

The standard Nichrome wire igniter is easily made. Take a piece of commercial Nichrome wire (available from model rocket companies) and wind the center section around a pencil point to form several very small loops. The wire now resembles a tiny filament from a light bulb. Insert the coiled section of the igniter in the nozzle of the engine until the coil is resting against the propellant grain. In other words, as far as it will go. Then take a small piece of cotton or soft paper tissue and tamp this in to hold the igniter in place. Have no fears about the tissue jamming in the nozzle during ignition. Very few traces will be found after the engine fires.

Several commercial types of igniters are available. One of these is the Sureshot. A diagram of this type is shown.

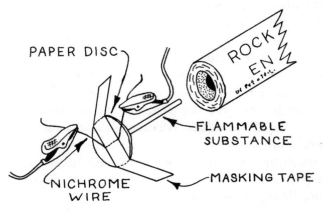

PAPER DISC

ROCK
EN

FLAMMABLE
SUBSTANCE

NICHROME
WIRE

MASKING TAPE

A Sureshot igniter (sold in kit form with all materials included).

Another is the Estes Nichrome Igniter. This consists of a piece of Nichrome wire coated with a flammable substance that ignites more easily than the propellant itself. There is no need to loop it. Just fold in half and tamp in. Until you become an expert at rolling plain old ordinary Nichrome wire, the commercial types will be much more reliable.

When launching large model rockets (engines D through F types) it is necessary to use a totally different type of ignition system. First of all, a large launch tower or extremely heavy rod is needed, at least 60 inches (or 1½ meters) long. Nichrome wire by itself won't work. Either a section of heavy fuse ignited by Nichrome wire or an *electric match* is needed.

The *electric match* contains several highly combustible components and is a very delicate piece of equipment. It should never be left exposed to the air because these components may oxidize in time. Some experiments show it may even be ignited by walkie-talkie frequencies at close range, so shut off all electronic instruments. When not in use, store it in a metal box. Installation is rather complicated and varies from manufacturer to manufacturer. Follow the instructions that come with a particular type to the letter.

The liquid-fuel rocket is a little more complicated than a solid-fuel one. Liquid propellant is kept under pressure until the moment of launch. At this time a plug in the nozzle can either be pulled out manually or may be triggered by an electrical element. This element is a very small piece of wire (not Nichrome) that melts when an electric current passes through it. Since this wire holds the nozzle in, once it is gone the rocket takes off.

You may be wondering where the electric current is coming from. As we mentioned before, the simple launch system consists of a battery, a 12-foot piece of double

A simple but powerful launcher. Power comes from two 6-volt Hot Shot batteries and eight D-size photoflash batteries (in square case to the left).

lamp cord, a toggle safety switch, and a launch button. The power comes from the battery. It should be at least 6 volts and high amp, which means four flashlight batteries won't be enough. At least four D-size *photoflash* batteries must be used. If you're going to launch more than once or twice a month, however, you'd better get a 6-volt lantern battery which is cheaper in the long run. When launching clustered engines, more voltage and amperage is needed.

A heavy-duty group launcher used when many rockets are launched in sequence.

In order to keep your launch system together, better mount it in a launch box. This can be made of either wood or metal and encloses the battery and electronic equipment. The front of the box is a panel on which is mounted the safety switch and launch button. Keep the *lead wire* (lamp cord) within easy reach. In more complicated launching systems, an automobile battery and several coils of wire leading to two or more launch pads is used. In this case, a rotary switch is thrown in with the safety switch and launch button on the panel. Such launchers are often used for groups because they can fire one rocket after another without interruption.

When attaching the lead wire to the igniter a type of clip is used. This is commonly a *micro-clip* or small alligator clip. However, battery clips and even paper clips have been used successfully. Simply solder these to the ends of the lead wire.

A set procedure must be followed when launching model rockets. We suggest the following:

1. Install the igniter in the engine of the rocket.
2. Slip the rocket on the launch rod or in the tower.
3. Making sure all switches are OFF and no current is flowing, attach lead wires to the igniter by means of clips.
4. Get at least 10 feet away from the launch pad and throw the safety switch on.
5. After at least a 5-second countdown, press the launch button to launch the rocket.
6. Immediately after launch turn safety switch OFF.

Now, what has happened if you press the launch button and nothing happens?

a. Your battery is too weak.
b. There is a short somewhere in the launch system.
c. The igniter burned through without igniting the propellant.
d. A freak condition has occurred.

First, check (c). If the igniter is burned through, the wire was not in contact with the propellant grain. Install another igniter. If the igniter's okay, check for any shorts (b). Shorts are most commonly caused by the micro-clips shorting out against the blast deflector. Also, if the igniter crosses over itself a short will result. Proper precautions will keep this from happening again. Of course, there is always a possibility of a short within the launch circuits— a broken toggle switch, for instance. Check this.

A high-capacity launch rack.

There are only a few possible culprits left. One is the battery (a). Simply attach the lead wires directly to the battery bypassing all switches and see if a test igniter (that is, not in an engine) glows red hot. If it doesn't, get a new battery.

Beware of a freak condition, however (d). Sometimes a lead wire will break inside its insulation. This can be detected by running the wire through your fingers and feeling for it.

Another possibility is dirty or improperly connected micro-clips. To prevent this, sand lightly after each launch the portion of the clip that contacts the igniter. Make sure the igniter is firmly in the jaws of the micro-clip before launch.

In addition to all this, safety precautions must be taken to avoid possible injury to spectators and bystanders. Never launch with anyone except the recovery crew in the expected recovery area. If a parachute fails to open the crew will know what to do, but a bystander won't. No one should be less than 10 feet from the launch pad during countdown and ignition. Unless protected by some kind of shield—a car, for example—everyone should be on his feet in case a rocket goes wild. Also, the FAA doesn't like the idea of your shooting down airplanes or even scaring pilots and passengers. If there is any aircraft in the immediate vicinity (including model aircraft), do not launch until the sky is clear.

CHAPTER 5

What goes on up there?

What causes a model rocket to loop in the air and crash into the ground? What makes a rocket go up only 500 feet instead of the expected 5000? It's the stuff we breathe —air.

If you flip a pencil into the air, it spins around a certain point. This is called the *center of gravity* (CG). A practical method of finding the CG is simply to balance the rocket on the edge of a knife or ruler. It is at the point of balance—the center of gravity—that all gravitational forces take effect on your rocket.

Now assume your rocket has uniform weight. To approximate this, cut an outline out of stiff cardboard exactly in the shape of your rocket. Now find the balance point of this by using the old knife or ruler trick. This is the lateral *center of pressure* (CP). All aerodynamic forces act through this point.

Remember, the lateral center of pressure is not the true center of pressure. It is, however, a close enough approximation for the beginner to use. Finding the true CP takes plenty of mathematical calculations. Technical reports describing in detail how to do this are listed in the Selected Readings at the back of the book.

In order for a rocket to be stable, the center of pressure must be toward the tail, behind the center of gravity. If the CP and CG are in the same spot, the rocket will

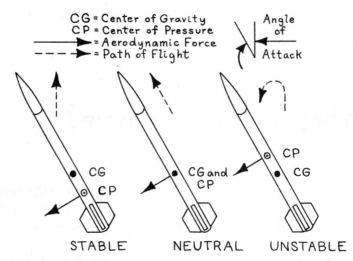

CG and CP placement in a model rocket and the resulting stability.

have neutral stability. When CP is ahead of CG, instability results.

The accompanying diagram shows the relative positions of CP and CG, not necessarily to scale.

Theoretically, if a rocket points exactly straight up it will always be stable. Practically, this never occurs. There's always at least a small *angle of attack*. The angle of attack is the number of degrees the rocket deviates from the vertical.

A rocket always has a tendency to rotate around its CG. In a typical rocket in flight and under thrust, the aerodynamic forces have a tendency to pull toward the ground through the CP. When the angle of attack develops, the rocket will tip in some direction. If the CP is behind the CG, it is immediately pulled back by aerodynamic forces. Thus the rocket keeps on going straight up.

If the rocket is neutrally stable, then it's like your pencil —the CP and the CG are in the same place. As your rocket

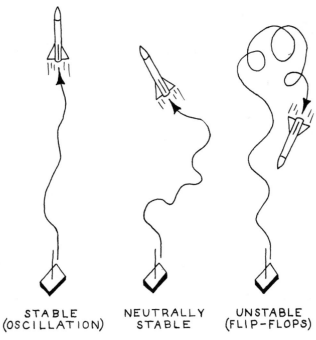

STABLE   NEUTRALLY   UNSTABLE
(OSCILLATION)   STABLE   (FLIP-FLOPS)

Types of stability.

is moving through the air, the angle of attack simply changes its course. There is no correcting force. As the wind blows, so goes your rocket. It is literally an uncontrolled flight.

Now let's assume the CP is ahead of the CG. When the angle of attack forms, the aerodynamic forces tend to pull the rocket upside down. This reverses the direction of motion of the rocket and the whole thing happens all over again. Your rocket flip-flops. It's quite spectacular but, especially if this occurs close to the ground, a little nerve-wracking too.

If the rocket checks out as being unstable, there are two things you can do: move the CP backward or move the CG forward. The size of the fins determines the placement of the CP if the body diameter of the rocket does not vary. Therefore, the easiest way to shift the CP backward is by making larger fins. The CG is moved forward easily too. Just add weight to the nose or put in a heavier payload.

During flight the CG varies according to the amount of propellant still left unburned in the engine. The rocket, therefore, becomes more stable as the flight progresses. This can have severe consequences. The rocket may start off by being unstable and then suddenly become stable halfway through the flight. After doing flip-flops around the sky, the rocket could very well be pointing toward the ground when it suddenly stabilizes and dives into anything underneath at full power.

The CP can also change due to wind, humidity, and many other factors. For this reason, declare a rocket stable only if the CP is at least one half the body diameter behind the CG to provide a margin of safety.

Don't try to make your rocket super-stable. The more stable a rocket is, the more it is apt to *weathercock*. Weathercocking is the tendency for a rocket to nose into the wind, and the wind may be blowing from undesirable directions.

Theoretically, the altitude of a model rocket is expected to be 10,000 feet. Actually, it only goes up 2500. What happened?

The answer is the force of *drag*. Drag may have several causes. The obvious one is the friction of the air on the surface of the rocket itself. But other things add up too: drag on launch lugs, fins, the nose cone and body itself; air turbulence at fins and at fin joints; and our old friend the angle of attack. These factors add up to a hefty force quite capable of sapping most of the strength of your rocket engine.

Drag can be reduced but never eliminated. Smooth, symmetrical airfoils on fins, glasslike finishes, fins angled downward instead of at right angles, and high stability to reduce increasing angle of attack all help. In fact, a rocket that doesn't follow any of these precautions may have drag forces that sap up to 90 per cent of the drag-free potential altitude.

Douglas J. Malewicki[1] has developed a method of estimating the effects of drag on altitude calculations in three phases of flight—during thrusting, during coasting after engine burnout, and in second or subsequent stages of firing. With his modified algebraic formulas, altitudes may be estimated very accurately. Before this, hours of repetitive computation or computer work were needed to make any kind of accurate estimate.

To understand and use the formulas, some simple preliminary work is necessary. Many factors influence the eventual altitude a rocket will actually reach, and they can cut the theoretical drag-free height of flight to less than half—for example, from 1900 to 700 feet in the case of some models. These factors include the size of the frontal area of the rocket exposed to colliding air molecules, the shape and surface smoothness of the rocket, the weight of the rocket (the force of earth's gravity), the amount of engine propellant burned off during thrust, and many more.

To simplify calculations for all of these variables, you can begin by assuming that the typical model rocket will have a drag coefficient of three quarters (.75). This coefficient is a measure of how easily a given shape will pass through air molecules, and it remains constant regardless of the size of that shape. To obtain the precise drag

[1] Douglas J. Malewicki, *Model Rocket Altitude Prediction Charts Including Aerodynamic Drag*, Estes Industries, Technical Report No. TR-10, 1967.

coefficient for various shapes of finished and unfinished nose cones regardless of size, you would have to conduct extensive wind tunnel tests. However, since this is impractical for most model rocketeers, the approximate guess of .75 will work for most of your models.

The drag coefficient does vary slightly with turbulence, launch site altitude, temperature of air, and angle of attack. If you want to take these conditions into account, both Malewicki (on pages 3 and 4 of his report) and Stine (in his *Handbook* on page 94)[2] provide further information.

Knowing the drag coefficient (C_d) for your rocket, a "typical" model, you can now calculate the ballistic coefficient (B):

$$B = \frac{W}{C_d \times A}$$

where W = weight *in ounces*
A = frontal area exposed to air drag *in square inches*

During the thrusting phase of flight, the *average* weight is used. This equals the initial weight of the rocket minus one half the engine propellant weight. For all practical purposes, the frontal area of your rocket is considered to be the area of a cross section of the body tube ($3.14 \times \text{radius}^2$).

One final preliminary calculation for the drag-free acceleration (a) is necessary:

$$a = (\frac{T}{W} - 1) \text{ in } gs \text{ of acceleration}$$

where W = weight *in ounces*
$$T = \frac{\text{total impulse of engine}}{\text{burn time}} = \text{thrust } in \text{ ounces}$$

[2] G. Harry Stine, *Handbook of Model Rocketry*, 2nd ed. Chicago: Follett, 1967.

The ballistic coefficient and the drag-free acceleration are all you need, together with the tables in Appendix 2, to utilize Malewicki's formulas, which contain the following symbols and terminology:

a=drag-free acceleration
B=ballistic coefficient
S=altitude in feet
t=time in seconds
V=velocity in feet per second
b as a subscript referring to burnout
c as a subscript referring to coasting
1 as a subscript referring to first stage
2 as a subscript referring to second stage
cos=cosine
cosh=hyperbolic cosine
ln=natural logarithm
sinh=hyperbolic sine
tan=tangent
$\tan^{-1}$=arc tangent
tanh=hyperbolic tangent
$\tanh^{-1}$=arc hyperbolic tangent

(Malewicki has already included values for two constants: sea level density of air and earth's gravitational force.)

Calculations for Thrusting Phase of Flight

1. To find the thrust altitude as a function of time:

$$S=235 \times B \times \ln \cosh \left(.37 \times \frac{\sqrt{a}}{\sqrt{B}} \times t\right)$$

2. To find the thrust velocity as a function of time:

$$V=87 \times \sqrt{B} \times \sqrt{a} \times \tanh \left(.37 \times \frac{\sqrt{a}}{\sqrt{B}} \times t\right)$$

Note that when time (t) equals motor burnout time (t_b), the altitude (S) equals burnout altitude (S_b) and the velocity (V) equals burnout velocity (V_b).

Calculations for Coasting Phase of Flight

1. To find the coast altitude (S_c), which is the distance traveled between the time of engine burnout and the time at which the rocket reaches its peak altitude:

$$S_c = 118 \times B \times \ln\ (1 + \frac{V_b^2}{7660 \times B})$$

2. To find the coast time (t_c), which is the time it takes the rocket to slow down to zero velocity $(V=0)$ and reach the peak of flight before beginning to fall back toward earth:

$$t_c = 2.7 \times \sqrt{B} \times \tan^{-1}\ (\frac{V_b}{87 \times \sqrt{B}})$$

3. To find the distance traveled at any time between burnout and peak altitude as a function of time:

$$S = S_c + 235 \times B \times \ln\ \cos\ (.37 \times \frac{t_c - t}{\sqrt{B}})$$

4. To find the coast velocity (V_c) as a function of time from engine burnout:

$$V_c = 87 + \sqrt{B} \times \tan\ (.37 \times \frac{t_c - t}{\sqrt{B}})$$

Calculations for Second and Subsequent Stages of Firing

1. To find the altitude gained as a function of time from burnout of the previous stage:

$$S_2 = 235 \times B \times \ln \left[\cosh\ (.37 \times \frac{\sqrt{a}}{\sqrt{B}} \times t) + \frac{V_{b1}}{87 \times \sqrt{B} \times \sqrt{a}} \right.$$

$$\left. \times \sinh\ (.37 \times \frac{\sqrt{a}}{\sqrt{B}} \times t) \right]$$

2. To find the velocity of the second (or third) stage as a function of time from burnout of the previous stage:

$$V_{b_2} = 87 \times \sqrt{B} \times \sqrt{a} \times \tanh\left[.37 \times \frac{\sqrt{a}}{\sqrt{B}} \times t + \tanh^{-1}\left(\frac{V_{b1}}{87 \times \sqrt{B} \times \sqrt{a}}\right)\right]$$

Note that when time (t) equals burnout time (t_b) for this stage that the altitude (S_2) becomes the second (or third) stage burnout altitude (S_{b_2}) and the velocity becomes the second (or third) stage burnout velocity (V_{b_2}).

Dave Moon, a model rocketeer in Wayland, Massachusetts, has determined altitude, velocity, and acceleration of various rocket types (by $C_d \times A$) with different engines on the computer, utilizing these formulas. His charts appear in Appendix 3. A good model rocket experimental project would be the testing of Dave's calculations by actual flight.

CHAPTER 6

Recovery

Designing a rocket that will come down is no trick. Controlling the *velocity* at which it plunges earthward, however, takes a recovery system. Recovery systems are used for two reasons: one, to prevent clobbering people or objects on the ground and, two, to enable you to fly your rocket again and again. Rockets are cheap, but we have yet to see a rocketeer who doesn't flinch when his model splinters on impact with the ground.

The basic purpose of a recovery device is to get your rocket from up there to down here safely. The kind of recovery system depends on the size and purpose of the rocket. Tumble, engine ejection, and so-called "featherweight" systems are for small (under 6 inches, or 15 centimeters), high altitude, inexpensive sport models. Larger single-stagers may use nose-blow, streamers, or parachutes. Cluster rockets and payload models nearly all use one to four large parachutes. Then, of course, there are rockets designed for a particular type of recovery such as boost-gliders. Less well known are helicopter and breakup recovery systems.

Tumble recovery involves shifting the center of gravity behind the center of pressure. As you now know, this makes a rocket unstable, a bad condition for powered flight but great for recovery. The rocket "tumbles" end over end, creating a large amount of drag. This drag slows down the rocket to acceptable speeds.

For tumble recovery the nose cone is glued solidly on the body tube. When the ejection charge fires, the engine is forced back where it is caught by a wire or metal hook. With the weight shifted to the tail, the rocket is unstable. The first model rocket to be brought out in kit form, Estes' Astron Scout, was based on this principle.

Engine ejection is also based on a CG shift. In this case, the engine is completely ejected from the rocket. It's connected to a screw eye in the nose cone by means of a shock cord, however. In this way the rocket tends to descend tail first.

"Featherweight" simply means the engine casing is blown out and the rocket falls to earth. The principle here is weight. As long as the rocket weighs ¼ ounce (about 7 grams) or less, neither the rocket nor anything it hits will be damaged. In other words, it's a system suitable for birds as light in weight as a feather.

The simplest recovery system for medium size rockets is nose-blow. At the apex of flight, the nose cone detaches from the body tube (still connected with a shock cord, of course) and the aerodynamically unstable pieces float to the ground.

More common than nose-blow is streamer recovery. The object in using a streamer is not so much to increase air resistance as to make the rocket more visible than it is with plain nose-blow. Streamers are made from crepe paper, cloth, or plastic and are usually a yard (about 1 meter) or so long.

Roll the streamer tightly to fit in the body tube so as to prevent its being damaged or tangled. When the ejection charge goes off, it pushes the streamer, shock cord, and nose cone out of the body tube, thus deploying a recovery system that will enable lightweight rockets to descend fairly slowly.

Parachutes are used as recovery systems because they offer medium to large rockets a slow descent and a smooth landing. A parachute may be made of plastic as well as of

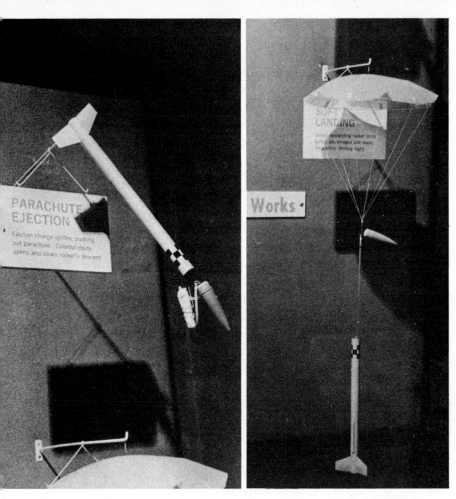

Parachute ejection and recovery from an exhibit at the Smithsonian Institution, Washington, D.C.

silk, nylon, or tough rice paper. They vary in size from 10 to 40 inches (or 25 centimeters to 1 meter) in diameter and in shape from square to round. The parachute is attached to the nose cone by shroud lines made of strong cotton or nylon cord. These lines are taped to the parachute and the opposite ends tied to the screw eye on the nose cone.

Parachutes must deploy successfully in order to work. To begin with, the parachute must be packed correctly. First, open the parachute and spread it out. If it is plastic, sprinkle talcum powder on both sides. Then grasp the shroud lines in one hand and the peak of the parachute in the other and pull gently, forming a cone. Now, starting at the top, roll the parachute as tight as possible until the shroud lines are reached. Don't wind the shroud lines around the rolled parachute—just leave them loose. The parachute cannot be tangled in any way. Now the parachute should deploy immediately after ejection.

Don't forget that the ejection charge has a power all its own. To prevent charring and melting, flameproof tissue or cotton should be placed between the engine and the parachute. In order to be effective, make sure the depth of the wadding is about 1½ times the diameter of the body tube.

Liquid-fuel model rockets use parachute recovery. After the rocket's fuel is nearly used up, some of the gas goes forward and leaks through a timer *disc* and activates the *separator*. Pressure leaks out slowly through the timer disc (a thin piece of paper) to allow the rocket time to coast to its peak. When it does, the clamps in the separator that hold the parachute tube on the engine loosen causing the parachute to fall out. In this case, the parachute must not be packed tightly and should be free to drop out when the parachute tube is held vertically.

A glide recovery system is basic to boost-gliders, which are specially designed for this purpose. Boost-gliders ascend vertically after powered flight, then glide to earth in much the same way nickel gliders and paper airplanes do. Construction of boost-gliders takes a fair amount of skill. To fly correctly, the glider must be well-balanced and made with precision. For this reason, Chapter 9 deals with boost-gliders.

All recovery systems are based on at least one of three

principles: change in stability (nose-blow and streamer), airbrake (parachute), and glide. There are combinations—a very large streamer or extremely small parachute, for example, would be both a change in stability and an airbrake.

Larger, heavier rockets need heavy-duty recovery systems. With the exception of a few isolated boost-glider designs, the only effective device for a large rocket is a parachute. Paper and plastic are usually not strong enough for rockets heavier than 2 ounces (or 56 grams). If only one parachute is used, silk or Mylar is the recommended material. If you use several parachutes, watch to see the shroud lines don't become tangled.

Some model rockets have their recovery systems incorporated into their designs. One has flaps on each fin which flip up tabs when the ejection charge fires. The rocket then "helicopters" down to earth. Another rocket is made of a ridged paper cone and so is a type of parachute in itself.

If it's any comfort to you, what goes up must come down. Where it comes down is another matter. Watch out for high winds, trees, telephone poles and wires, glass houses, spectators in the recovery area, and low-flying aircraft.

CHAPTER 7

Staging and clustering

Our astronauts at Cape Kennedy are not launched in one-engine, single-stage rockets. If they were, they would go about 50 miles straight up and another 50 straight down. Several engines, however, manage very well.

Model rockets follow the same principles. If you want to reach higher altitudes and lift heavier payloads cheaply, more than one engine is needed. There are two ways to do this in model rocketry: *staging* and *clustering*.

Staging is simple enough. A typical two-stage rocket consists of one part called the *sustainer* and another called the *booster*. The booster, or first stage, is ignited first. When thrust stops, a sustainer, or second stage, ignites and the booster returns to earth.

In order to ignite the second stage, the end of the booster engine must be taped to the nozzle of the sustainer engine. Booster engines have no delay or ejection charge. When nearly all the propellant in the booster engine is burned, the remaining amount blows out the forward end in a mass of hot sparks and gases. These gases then enter the nozzle of the sustainer engine and ignite it. When the sustainer engine ignites, the force of the exhaust quickly blows the booster free to return to the ground. The reason the engines are taped together is to make sure all the sparks and gases get into the nozzle of the sustainer engine. Otherwise ignition would only occur about half the time.

A two-stage rocket.

SINGLE BURNING ENGINE:

SPACE

CERAMIC NOZZLE

PROPELLANT

STAGING:

PROPELLANT WALL RUPTURES
FLAMING PARTICLES IGNITE 2ND STAGE

Second-stage ignition.

Multistage rockets are not restricted to just two stages. Three stages are common and four have been successfully flown too. When more than four are used, however, the small unreliability factor inherent in all multistage models is vastly increased.

One problem is that of stability. When stability checks are made, first check for the top stage, then for the top two stages, the top three stages, and so on. If this is not done, you may end up with a stable two-stage rocket but an unstable one-stage rocket. Unfortunately, there are disadvantages to good stability too. Every model rocket has a tendency to weathercock into the wind. Two-stage rockets double this tendency. You can imagine what four, five, or six might do!

Before we knew this, we sent a beautiful four-stage rocket up into a light breeze. By the time the second stage fired, it was pointing horizontally to the ground. We then had the joyful experience of watching the other three stages push it off into the sunset (and a swamp) miles away.

Another important thing to watch in attempting to stabilize your rocket is the weight in the tail. This puts the center of gravity behind a lot of fins if you're not careful. If you want your rocket to paint figure eights across the sky, try it. But if you want it to go straight up, be sure there is sufficient payload up front.

Just for the record, a multistage model weighs a lot more than the average sport model. Therefore the engines have to be powerful, especially in the booster stages. Otherwise your rocket may rise 10 feet and fall to the ground.

Booster engines have a zero where the delay designation is in the classification. For example, B14–0 would be a booster engine whereas B14–7 could be used for the sustainer.

How do you make a booster? Take a section of body tube as long as the engine that will be used. If the diameter of the body tube is considerably larger than the diameter of the engine, glue an engine mount in the section. Otherwise, an engine block will be enough.

Next, glue the fins on the booster. Fins should be especially large. The reason is apparent when you start the stability checks. The center of pressure must be substantially behind the center of gravity at all times. Experiment and see exactly what size fins are needed for your design. Attach the fins very securely to the booster. If a fin comes off on a booster, the rocket tips earthward and chances are it will strike under full power from one of its other stages.

The sustainer is a snap to make. All it is is a common single-stage model such as we've been talking about from the beginning. The only difference is that the sustainer engine must have an especially long delay because it has to coast from the acceleration of more than one engine. To determine mathematically what the exact coast time will be, check

Douglas Malewicki's calculations in Chapter 5. This is only if you want near perfect performance, however.

Launching multistage models presents a few special problems. Unless the fins of each stage are aligned, a tower is out of the question. If a launch rod or rail is used there should be a lug on each stage. If you don't do this, you may end up with one booster peeling off on its own or the rocket jackknifing in midair.

In any case, an especially long initial guidance system is needed. Launch rods, towers, and rails should be at least 3 and probably 4 to 6 feet (about 1 to 2 meters) long. This is because the increased weight of the rocket prevents quick initial lift-off.

The disadvantage to staging is that a fairly hefty payload cannot be budged. The rocket weighs more itself and if a large payload is used too, the booster lacks the power to get the rocket to stabilizing velocity. In this case, you have a neutrally stable rocket for half the flight with the obvious disastrous consequences. For this reason, another way of using more than one engine has been developed: clustering.

Clustering consists of two to four engines being ignited simultaneously. Thus the duration of burning is not affected, but you get much more thrust. Three engines have three times the total impulse whether they are ignited separately or at the same time. However, with a heavy payload one engine may not have the power to lift it effectively whereas three at once will manage quite well.

Many of the stability problems inherent in staging are also problems in clustering. All the weight is again in the tail. This is not that much of a problem because clustering is used almost exclusively to lift heavy payloads. This payload weight will usually move the center of gravity sufficiently forward, but be sure and check this out. In the event that it isn't, a large rocket with many times the thrust of a sport rocket will be thrashing around your head.

Two payload cluster rockets. Payload in the rocket on the left is an egg.

A long rocket is naturally easier to stabilize than a short rocket. Don't be afraid to lengthen your rocket by a couple of feet even though it may seem unnecessary.

However, because of the extended body tubes in some clustered models, the force of even two or three ejection charges may not be sufficient to deploy a parachute of the size needed to return the rocket safely to earth. This problem is solved easily by gluing a "stuffer tube" in the model rocket. All this is is a small diameter body tube encircled at both ends by a balsa or paper block that guides the exhaust gases forward and concentrates them.

Another necessary precaution is making sure all engines are securely held in the rocket. If an engine is ejected when the ejection charge fires, the pressure will escape through the rear of the rocket and the recovery system won't be deployed.

Don't skimp on parachutes. You've got a heavy rocket there, and a little 12-incher isn't going to do much good. In addition, two, three, or four parachutes may be needed if a large payload is included.

Thrust may not always be absolutely constant among all of the clustered engines. It may be slightly off-center now and then during flight. In order to prevent a serious loss of altitude, a small amount of spin may be induced. This can be accomplished by non-symmetrical airfoil, canted fins, or very small spin tabs. Just don't overdo it. Also, if you're sending up a camera, don't intentionally induce spin or you'll just get a blurry picture. If you're sending up an insect, you could get an airsick cricket.

Cluster rockets are relatively easy to construct. The trick is to launch them. First of all, you need a lot of power. A couple of 6-volt lantern batteries or a 12-volt automobile battery is minimum for two to four engines. Remember you have to ignite one igniter per engine simultaneously. One igniter can't fire even one-quarter second after another. If

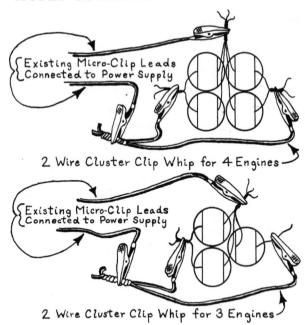

Existing Micro-Clip Leads
Connected to Power Supply

2 Wire Cluster Clip Whip for 4 Engines

Existing Micro-Clip Leads
Connected to Power Supply

2 Wire Cluster Clip Whip for 3 Engines

Cluster igniter wiring.

this does happen and one or more engines fail to ignite, the rocket will veer way off course.

Extra care should be used preparing igniters. Be absolutely positive the igniters are touching the propellant grain. We recommend, in any case, that four engines be the maximum number used for clustering. Anything over that and the reliability is just too small.

Launching requires a special wiring setup. An extra micro-clip must be connected to one terminal. The easiest way to do this is to take a 4-inch piece of wire (lamp cord) and attach a micro-clip to both ends. Then scrape the insulation off in the middle. Whenever you need the extra micro-clip, simply attach it permanently on your launch system at the spot where the insulation has been scraped off.

You've probably been wondering why you couldn't have a combination of staging and clustering in a model rocket. You can, but only to a certain extent. Only the first stage may be clustered. If two or more engines are connected together as described in the first part of the chapter, one engine in the second stage could very well ignite before the others because of the inconsistencies in rocket engine design.

A single-engine booster may be allowed to tumble back to earth but a clustered booster is too heavy and should have its own separate recovery system. The simplest is a small parachute since only one engine of the cluster is needed to ignite the next engine in line; one of the other engines may have a short delay in the ejection which could deploy the parachute.

The main difference between clustering and staging in ordinary model rockets is that all the problems involved in plain model rocketry are magnified. Higher altitudes are reached, so make sure no airplanes are in sight, model or otherwise. As these rockets are heavier, make sure no bystander gets hit. You can't afford even an occasional instability with rockets of this size and power.

CHAPTER 8

Hornets, eggs, and other payloads

Our first attempt at sending up a payload was a disaster, not because our rocket failed to function properly but because of the rather neurotic passenger. Let us say here and now we categorically do not recommend hornets! In other words, we had barely started and already payload rocketry was beginning to bug us.

Insects are not the only payloads waiting to be launched. They have an advantage in being readily available and your kid sister is less likely to be emotionally involved with a bug than with something more substantial such as a mouse. There's really no point in sending up mice, frogs, or higher animals (that includes the kid sister too). The acceleration and jolts would be too much and you could end up with a dead animal.

Raw eggs, being expendable, are frequently launched instead of live payloads. Keeping one from breaking in flight presents a certain challenge. Also the payload capsule must be carefully constructed to avoid showering the launch personnel. Once you launch two eggs in a row without damage, you can consider yourself ready to move on to more difficult things.

You've probably been puzzled about how you put the pay-

load on the rocket. This is done with a *payload capsule.*
A payload capsule may be constructed in several ways. The
easiest to make consists of a section of body tube capped
with a nose cone and based with a balsa block or balsa re-
ducer.

Special types of payload capsules include ones designed
to be the actual fronts of the rocket, such as some rocket
cameras. Clear plastic payload tubing is sometimes used
instead of just a plain body tube. This enables you to
check out your payload without removing the nose cone
just before flight and during countdown.

Since most payloads are heavy, separate recovery systems
are used for the payload capsule and the rest of the rocket.
This is usually done with two parachutes. The body tube
and payload capsule are still attached together by a shock
cord to prevent the two from becoming separated during
recovery and also as a safety measure in case one parachute
fails.

As far as stability goes, most payload models are very
steady in flight. The extra weight in the nose section of the
rocket causes a huge shift in the center of gravity ahead
of the center of pressure. For this reason, smaller fins producing less drag may be used. However, watch out for the
rocket that is stable with the payload and unstable without
it. When making stability checks, be sure your model is
okay with no weight in the nose.

You're probably wondering what kinds of engines to use.
The answer is: powerful ones. Anything under B total-im-
pulse would be disastrous if your payload weighs more
than 1 ounce (or 30 grams). For anything as heavy as an
egg, the more powerful C through F class engines should be
used. Refer to the engine classifications on page 24 in
Chapter 3. A word of warning about engines: check to see
what the maximum thrust is. One commercial engine has
more than 100 newtons of thrust which causes, to say the

least, exceedingly high acceleration. Any egg or loosely constructed electronic equipment would be crushed instantly. Generally, the best kind of engines to use are end burners with medium thrust and long duration.

Since payload rockets have so much weight, their inertia is fantastic at burnout. To put it simply, your rocket will coast for a long time after thrust stops. Therefore, long delays are usually needed. There are exceptions, of course. One would be a fairly heavy rocket with a rather weak engine. A long delay in this case would cause the rocket to nose over and plunge to earth moving at a good clip when the ejection charge fired. In all probability this would rip any recovery system to shreds.

There are some basic precautions that must be taken with all kinds of payloads. The payload capsule should always be padded to prevent damage at lift-off and the shock of landing. It should be well put together, with all parts fitting tightly. Someone on the ground is going to be awfully surprised if your payload dumps out without a parachute at the apogee of flight. The recovery system should be carefully checked out. A 1-ounce (or 30-gram) model rocket probably won't be damaged too much if it hits the ground after its parachute fails to open, but a 3-ounce (or 90-gram) payload capsule will plunge like a rock and completely splinter on impact, splintering anything inside, too.

Now we'll talk about some different kinds of payloads.

A new and popular development in model rocketry is the rocket camera for taking aerial photos. The camera payload will cost you about $4.00 and there is an easy-to-assemble kit on the market. Film comes in individual discs. When loaded in the camera, each disc is good for one shot only. The shutter is triggered by the ejection charge, and engines with excessive delays are used so the rocket is pointing toward the ground when the charge goes off. You then get an

Aerial photos from a model rocket still camera (Estes Industries Kit: *Camroc*).

aerial shot of whatever is underneath. Although originally limited to black and white, color photography is now practical too. Another recent development is the rocket movie camera.

Still very much in the experimental stage are radio transmitters. The reason this has not been developed more rapidly is that, although a transmitter may cost only about $20, several hundred dollars worth of ground equipment

is needed to receive and process the signal. Theoretically, these radio transmitters could be used to signal back information on acceleration, yaw, pitch and roll, and the shock of launching and recovery system deployment. Until someone perfects this method, we have to rely on self-contained instruments.

One of these instruments is the *accelerometer*. Not surprisingly, this is used to measure maximum acceleration. This is actually a simple gadget consisting of a small piece of wax paper, a spring of known compressibility, and a small metal weight and stylus.

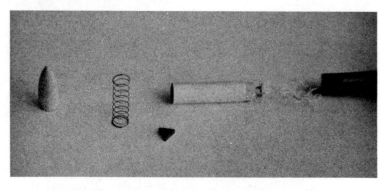

An inexpensive accelerometer (expanded view).

The wax paper lines the inside of the payload capsule. The spring, just a little smaller in diameter than the capsule itself, fits inside the wax paper. The weight and stylus are placed on top of the spring. When the rocket is launched, the weight and stylus are forced down by the acceleration and engrave the paper. If the weight of the stylus is known, and the compressibility of the spring is known, it becomes a simple matter to determine maximum acceleration.

For example, suppose you had a ¼-ounce (or 7-gram) stylus and a spring with a compressibility of 1 ounce per inch (or 28 grams per 2½ centimeters). If the spring is forced down 2 inches (or 5 centimeters) as shown on the wax paper, then the acceleration is 8 gs. This measure of acceleration just means that at the maximum any object in the payload capsule would appear to weigh eight times its normal amount. Model rocket companies sell accelerometer kits for about $2.00.

We can't cover every possible payload in one chapter—you probably have an idea of your own right now. Just be sure to stick with the basic precautions so you don't repeat the mistakes of hundreds of other model rocketeers in the past.

CHAPTER 9

Boost-gliders

A boost-glider means one thing to a model rocketeer and something else to a model airplane enthusiast. It is either (1) a model rocket with glide recovery, or (2) a glider with VTO (vertical take-off) boost.

Hold it! We know you're going to ask, "What's the bit about VTO? Why can't I make a rocket-powered airplane instead of a glider?"

Unfortunately, the HTO (horizontal take-off) jobs will have to be left to Jetex and carbon dioxide capsules. For the most part, model rocket engines are light in weight, have a short duration, and possess levels of thrust too high for any kind of successful "X-15" or "Bomarc" you might design. In fact, before 1961, many experiments were tried substituting A-type engines for Jetex in rocket-powered airplane kits.

The results were spectacular, but not in the way the experimenters had planned. *If* the wings didn't rip off, the aircraft behaved as you would expect any other rocket to— with the weight in the tail and the fins on the nose cone! There is just too much velocity for a standard airfoil. Anything the experimenters could develop looped, dove, yawed, pitched, rolled, and usually crashed to the ground. By the way, don't try to develop your own special airfoil. Tests would be necessary in a high-speed wind tunnel and extensive mathematical work would have to be done with computers and calculus.

Back to VTO, then. Boost-gliders (B/G) come in various shapes, sizes, styles, and functions. However, they may be divided into three main groupings: rear-engine, front-engine, and flex-wing.

The first glide-recovery model rocket was designed and built by John Schutz and Vernon Estes in 1961. This was a rear-engine boost-glider.

Rear-engine boost-glider and VTO (vertical take-off).

One of the greatest breakthroughs in model rocketry was the development of the front-engine boost-glider by Larry Renger. It looks very much like a standard hand-launched type. Renger models are better gliders because of this basic aerodynamic similarity and consequently are dominating competition in NAR and international meets.

Flex-wing boost-gliders are exactly what their name implies. They are made in such a way as to fold up and may be placed in the body tube like a recovery system. When the ejection charge fires, it blows out the whole complex. This unfolds and glides back to earth. There is no engine attached and the main body must be recovered by streamer or parachute. Flex-wing gliders are hard to trim and do not usually have as good flight characteristics as other B/G. For this reason they are seldom used in competition.

Boost-gliders have two natural phases of flight, boost and glide. Your boost-glider must be able to ascend vertically *and* glide back. With flex-wing B/G, you don't have to worry about the problems of VTO, but in all other types of B/Gs there is no way to avoid the worry. This means you must change the aerodynamic structure of the model at the apex of flight. This may be done by means of movable wing surfaces, variable geometry, canard surfaces that have rudders or flaps forward of the wing, or simply a shift in the center of gravity when the engine is ejected. Some B/Gs even go into an automatic glide at engine burnout, working on the off-center thrust principle.

Many of these B/G types are sold as commercial kits, and we recommend that you build several of them to help acquaint yourself with the aerodynamic principles involved before designing your own B/G. We didn't. As a result, one design started out as glide recovery and ended up "flutter" recovery. In other words, both wings came off and the body tube roared on to new heights while all the pieces floated down separately.

A front-engine boost-glider.

In order for a B/G to act like a rocket—VTO—the lifting surfaces must not affect the flight path in any way other than stabilizing like fins. In other words, the wings can't produce lift during powered flight. If they do—disaster results.

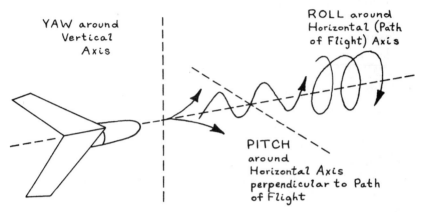

YAW around Vertical Axis

ROLL around Horizontal (Path of Flight) Axis

PITCH around Horizontal Axis perpendicular to Path of Flight

Three types of rotation around axes for a model rocket glider in flight.

Every model rocket rotates around three axes: yaw, pitch, and roll. Roll is easily corrected by using a *dihedral angle* between 15 and 20 degrees (see the diagram on page 84) and yaw usually can be eliminated by making the rudder area equal to 7 to 10 per cent of the wing area. These two are easy to control.

The pitch axis is another story, however. This is the biggest problem due to the fact that the wings and the stabilizer lie in that plane. During boost the model will pitch, loop, or both if it is not designed, constructed, or balanced with this axis in mind. During glide, the model may stall and spiral or act like any normal fin-stabilized model rocket and streamline into the ground.

If the pitch axis is to be stable, there must be a *balance of forces*. This will be easier to understand if you look at the diagram on page 84. As you can see on the airfoil, the CG is located ahead of the CP during boost. You realize the CG and CP are in the same position as they are in your ordinary everyday stabilized model rocket. As we've seen, this is great for boost but impossible for glide. You can test this by tossing one of your rockets into the air and watching what happens. See what a great glider it is?

"All right," you say. "What do I do about it?"

First, the CP of any flat or symmetrical airfoil is located 25 per cent of the chord (the width of the wing) distant from the front of the wing. This location doesn't change even at angles of attack up to 15 degrees from the direction of flight. Very simply, the CP is a constant. It won't change. An airfoil with an unchanging CP, therefore, has a natural tendency to pitch down during glide. In order for the model to glide there has to be an equal and opposite force to correct this. A balance of forces, or *equilibrium*, must exist.

There are two ways to institute the necessary change from VTO to stable glide: (1) a change in the actual configuration of the model or (2) a change in the CG location.

There are several methods of changing the configuration of a B/G. Among them are using wings that fold during boost and unfold for glide and using front canard surfaces that are activated at the apex of flight. These methods are fairly complex and should not be attempted except by a rocketeer who is interested in considerable effort and experimentation.

By far the most common method of changing B/G configuration is using hinged flaps on the wings. These flaps are held straight by activating wires attached to the engine during boost. When the engine casing is ejected, the wires are released, and an elastic cord, running from the flaps to the wing, pulls the flaps up. This changes the B/G's aerodynamics so it will glide. NAR regulations do not permit model rocket engines to be jettisoned without a recovery device, so if you're going to enter your B/G in NAR sanctioned competition, tape a streamer (36 square inches minimum) to it. This may be folded and inserted in a paper clip or similar holder affixed to the rear end of the body tube.

Much work still has to be done in the area of alterable-configuration B/Gs. The beginner is usually better off if he builds models that work on the CG shift principle. For the most part these are front-engine models anyway and therefore usually better flyers.

As we have seen, the CG is ahead of the CP during boost. If this situation remains during glide, the model will pitch down. In the system described above, flaps flipped up to correct for this, by creating an opposite force and bringing about equilibrium. There is an alternative, however. If the CG is shifted back to about the center of the wing chord during glide phase, the model will be at equilibrium. However, there is one additional problem—most wing airfoils of this kind are inherently unstable, and the glider has a tendency to flip up and loop over.

Therefore, all CG-shift-principle B/Gs have a stabilizer (*stab,* for short) mounted at the aft end. A boost-glider utilizing this method is fairly easy to design and to operate since there are no moving parts. It is activated simply by the ejection of the power pod (described at the end of this chapter).

How can you build a B/G that will operate on the CG-shift principle? G. Harry Stine has formulated a simple set of design rules. These are listed below and illustrated in the diagrams on pages 84 and 85. For those of you who want to go heavy on mathematical calculations and develop optimum designs, see the books listed in the Selected Readings.

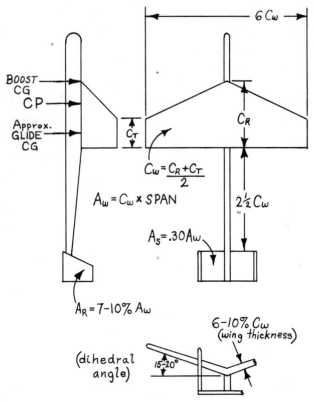

$6 C_W$

BOOST
CG

CP

Approx.
GLIDE
CG

C_T

C_R

$C_W = \dfrac{C_R + C_T}{2}$

$A_W = C_W \times SPAN$

$A_S = .30 A_W$

$2\tfrac{1}{2} C_W$

$A_R = 7\text{-}10\% A_W$

6-10% C_W
(wing thickness)

(dihedral
angle)

15-20°

G. Harry Stine's ratios for front-engine boost-gliders.

G. HARRY STINE'S BASIC DESIGN RULES FOR B/G

1. The wing span should be five to seven times the average wing chord (C_W). This means an aspect ratio (A.R.) of 5 to 7.
2. The wing should not be swept back more than 20 degrees; if it is, this condition creates high drag.
3. The thickness of the wing should be from 6 to 10 per cent of the average wing chord.
4. The stabilizer area (A_s) should be approximately one

third the wing area (A_W) and mounted *underneath* the fuselage. This is unlike the wings, which are mounted *on top*.

5. The distance between the *trailing* edge of the average wing chord and the *leading* edge of the stabilizer should be about 2.0 to 2.5 times the average wing chord.

6. Rudders may be mounted on the tips of the stabilizer instead of where they normally are on an airplane. This keeps the rudders out of the exhaust and also serves the dual purpose of preventing a tip vortex. This vortex causes high drag. The area of each rudder should be equal to about one twentieth the wing area, making a combined total rudder area (A_R) of from 7 to 10 per cent of the wing area.

7. As mentioned before, the wings should have a dihedral of 15 to 20 degrees to prevent roll.

8. Wings should be sanded into a lifting airfoil shape for best performance. The wing should be sanded flat on the bottom and have a rounded leading edge.

9. Your finished model should have a ratio of between 110 milligrams and 220 milligrams per square centimeter of wing area.

$$\text{AVERAGE WING CHORD} = \frac{C_1 + C_2}{2}$$

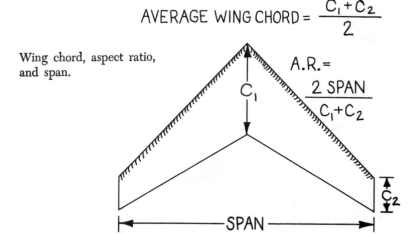

Wing chord, aspect ratio, and span.

$$\text{A.R.} = \frac{2 \text{ SPAN}}{C_1 + C_2}$$

C_1

C_2

SPAN

Follow these rules, and you will make a B/G that will glide effectively, and, if you have tested to make sure the CG is ahead of the CP during boost, one that will VTO effectively also. Don't worry about the airfoil shape of the fins; it will have very little effect on the vertical flight path of the model.

When constructing your model, don't make giant wings. The high thrust of most model rocket engines will simply rip them off. For any size wings, though, use a strong glue or epoxy and be sure to fillet. Don't ever use series-two, or port-burning, engines.

Wings are usually made from straight-grain balsa, although plastics and fiberglass are being tried experimentally. As with any substantial model rocket part, the wings should *always* be non-metallic.

Stabilizers and rudders should be made of the same stuff as the wings, and you should sand them into a standard streamlined *fin* airfoil as described in Chapter 2. The fuselage must be straight and strong. If the fuselage is made of balsa, then a ¼-inch×½-inch piece should be used for models up to 30 grams and a ¼-inch×¾-inch piece for 30 grams to 75 grams. These weights do not include the weight of the engine or power pod.

Some model rocketeers prefer not to finish their B/Gs and believe they will glide better if the surface is not smooth. We favor sealing, painting, and waxing the model as you would any model rocket. This will cut down drag, enabling it to travel higher during boost. Also, during glide, your model will be able to move at a higher velocity with the wings, thereby producing better lift.

After your B/G is built and finished, it should be tested. The best way to test your glider would be in a low-speed wind tunnel, but because few modelers have access to one (unless they belong to a club), your model will probably have to be tested in flight. These tests, fortunately, consist

simply of tossing your B/G and watching what happens.
If the model stalls, add weight in the form of small pieces
of wire or copper or lead strip to the nose. If it dives, weight
should be added to the tail or removed from the nose.
Don't throw your model hard or you may find yourself
building another one. Use just enough effort for a good
glide.

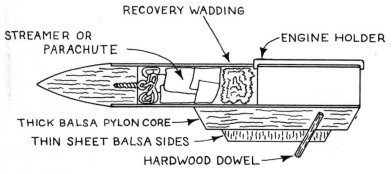

A B/G power pod.

Now add a power pod to your glider. The *pylon* of the
pod fits snugly in a groove cut in the fuselage. When the
ejection charges fires, the engine is slammed back where
it is caught by an engine holder. This force jerks the pod
off the fuselage leaving the glider in the sky. The ejection
charge also deploys a parachute, and the pod is recovered
separately.

So now you know about boost-gliders. Maybe you feel
they're good for practice in aerodynamics and have no real
purpose. But their uses are expanding. For example, a 45-
gram radio control device is now being developed for them.
NASA is concentrating on glide recovery as a means for
our astronauts to return to earth.

CHAPTER 10

Large-scale model rocketry

As the size and power of any rocket increases, the difficulties concerning its design and use increase also. Model rockets are no exception. A good rule, known as Larson's Law (after the model rocketeer who warned us), is that the difficulties increase by the square of the total impulse. While not exactly scientific, it holds true in an amazing number of cases.

You'll hear that there is no point to the larger models in view of the increased difficulties and cost. We feel the advantages of large-scale models are worth it. Let's look at what a D, an E, or an F engine can do.

The first thing any model rocketeer thinks about is altitude. We recently designed a model rocket using *one* E engine that tested out mathematically at more than 3280 feet. This is by no means exceptional either. Unfortunately for you altitude buffs, even a large model rocket begins to disappear from view at about 2500 feet. A high-magnification telescopic optical system with filters would be needed for tracking. You might even have to develop a type of radio telemetry system.

Because of these difficulties, large models are used most often to carry payloads. A 50-gram model rocket with a 450-gram payload (total mass: 500 grams) will easily hit 1000 feet with an F engine. Whole new fields are opened up

A large F-class payload model rocket.

with the additional total impulse power. Movie cameras, weather equipment, and other heavy and complex payloads have been launched this way.

Now let's take a look at the forces that affect large models.

Aerodynamic forces are massive on large models moving at high speed. You've noticed that professional rockets have nose cones in *true cone* shape. You know an ogive shape has less drag. Drag is proportional to the square of the velocity. At velocities from 600 fps to 700 fps (fps=feet per second) and on up, drag becomes proportional to velocity *cubed*. The whole compressibility of the air changes too. The air doesn't flow smoothly around an ogive; turbulence develops increasing drag. A cone, on the other hand, splits the air like a knife. Shock waves form and there is no extra drag due to turbulence.

Stability in large models is affected too. The center of pressure has a tendency to move around. Therefore, make sure the center of gravity is *several* body diameters ahead of the center of pressure.

In order to check out the velocity of your rocket on the drawing board, use the simplified equations at the end of Chapter 5. If the burnout velocity comes out to more than 700 fps, design and build with this in mind.

No matter what the velocity, because of the increased size and frontal area, fins should be cemented to the rocket with extra care. Epoxy is best if you know how to use it (read the instructions carefully) and gives a good strong joint. We've found four relatively small fins are better than three larger ones. Unless modeling plywood is used keep the fins small. Otherwise the "speed of balsa," the point when balsa construction collapses, could be reached, leaving you picking up the pieces.

It is absolutely essential that stability be determined *before flight*. And we mean *to the millimeter*. Your ½-

kilogram 1-meter rocket with a 9-second-thrust-duration F engine in it could be downright dangerous if it was unstable. Follow the instructions for determining stability in Chapter 5 carefully.

Now let's take a look at the part giving us all the problems: the large model rocket engines.

The first difficulty lies in the different dimensions of large D–F engines. Where 1/4A–C engines are, for the most part, the same size and standardized from company to company, the big ones are not. This makes it rough because a rocket can be designed around one particular engine only. There is no quick easy switching of engines to change the altitude and acceleration.

Besides the size, other data is also different. Duration, T-max, maximum and average thrust, total impulse, etc., varies with the company.

Building a large rocket is a long, hard, and fairly expensive job. Be sure you know exactly what engine you'll want to use, then plan around it. Chapter 5 has equations to determine this.

The structure of large model rockets is basically the same as for smaller rockets, but the construction has to be tougher. This includes body tubes, fins, engine mounts, and recovery systems.

Many diameters and lengths of body tubes are available. These are strong by themselves and need not be strengthened. Most are spiral-wound, however, and the resulting groove should be filled with balsa putty. This cuts down on drag and also improves the appearance of the model. If you don't want to use putty, brown paper tape (the kind you use to wrap packages) can be used instead. Just lick the gummed backing and paste in a continuous strip. When the body tube is covered, trim off the excess at both ends.

A body tube may also be covered with Silkspan, the material used in model airplanes. Although this adds great strength and provides a smooth low-drag surface, it is generally impractical for all but the most skilled modeler. Therefore it will not be discussed in this book. G. Harry Stine's *Handbook of Model Rocketry* does give instructions on pages 191–92.

Fins should be strong. The grain of the balsa *must not* run parallel to the body tube. It should always be parallel to the leading or trailing edge of the fin.

Fins should be small. A rocket with four fins will produce 33 per cent more fin drag than one with three fins of the same size. However, four fins result in greater stability. Therefore, fin size can be reduced when four are used to achieve the same drag as a three-fin rocket. In any case the increased strength and stability are worth it.

Attach fins either with epoxy or with plenty of glue fillets. The joint between the fin and the body tube is potentially the weakest. Be sure to sand the fins into a streamlined or rounded airfoil shape as shown on page 13.

Engines should always be mounted with an air space between them and the body tube. Large engines generate a terrific amount of heat, and this can bubble the paint job.

The last major thing to remember is the recovery system. Man, it has to be BIG! Except for a few special boost-gliders, parachutes are about the only practical devices for large rockets. Silk is most often used because there is a smaller chance of tearing or fusing.

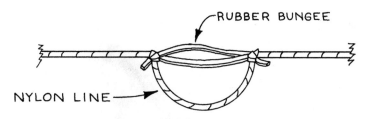

Rubber bungee strip for large rockets.

When attaching the shroud lines to the body tube use heavy cord. Always use a bungee strip, otherwise the shroud lines can snap or pull out of the body tube. At normal altitudes this is bad enough, but at high altitudes this will totally demolish your rocket.

Special instructions are included in Chapter 4 for launching large metal rockets. Don't just launch your big one from your present launcher. The safety precautions listed by individual manufacturers must be followed if large-scale model rockets are to be as safe as the small ones.

CHAPTER 11

Altitude and tracking

"Why bother with altitude math and complex theodolites?"

"Anyone can tell roughly how high it is, so why waste your time?"

"Who cares whether it went up 780 feet or 784 feet?"

"Just compare the flight to trees and telephone poles!"

Well, why not? Very simple. There's just too much limitation to the human eye. You may have 20/20 vision, but unless you have 80/20 vision you are not, repeat NOT, going to be able to even approximate the altitude your "bird" will go.

We know. Rockets we thought went at least 1000 feet traveled only half that height when checked out by theodolite. On the other hand, rockets we thought had reached 1500 feet have turned out to have gone up more than half a mile when checked. So you can see your eyes alone are not the answer to accurate altitude determination.

Comparing the flight of your rocket to the height of surrounding trees becomes pretty ridiculous when you consider that the world's tallest tree is only 385 feet tall, and that's a redwood in California. Unless you live in New York and can launch near the Empire State Building forget comparisons to surrounding buildings too.

"But," you say, "good tracking equipment costs hundreds of dollars!" True, but as we said before, no one needs to know the altitude within inches. Tracking devices certified by NAR and used at sectional, regional, and national meets cost as little as $30.00. This is still usually beyond the limits of an individual rocketeer's budget, however. Still, there are many other methods of finding, or at least estimating, the altitude of most model rockets.

One of the simplest methods of finding out which rocket goes higher is streamer duration. Introduced by Czechoslovakian modelers as a competition between two or more contestants, it can also be used as an accurate and valuable tool for the modeler in altitude design. All you need is a stop watch. Just launch any rocket fitted with streamer recovery and time the flight from the point of ignition to the moment of touchdown. Use a standard crepe paper streamer in all your rockets and use the same type engine. As mentioned, a standard streamer is 1 inch wide and 18 inches long. No other retarding devices may be used in the rocket. The point is, of course, that the higher a rocket gets, the longer the flight time.

The major drawback to streamer duration is that it is impossible to find the altitude without using calculus or to record any rockets other than those carrying streamers. For this reason inexpensive tracking devices are used by most modelers. The majority of beginning rocketeers shrink from altitude determination because the words imply algebra and trigonometry. It does, but only the basics. If you can read a table, multiply, and divide, you can calculate altitudes quickly, accurately, and easily.

A simple tracking device consists merely of a protractor bolted to a straight piece of wood and a string with a weight attached so the instrument registers 90 degrees when the tracker is in a horizontal position. At one end is a nail and at the other a screw eye constituting a simple sight. The weight holds the string taut so the angle of peak altitude may be calculated by subtracting 90 degrees from the

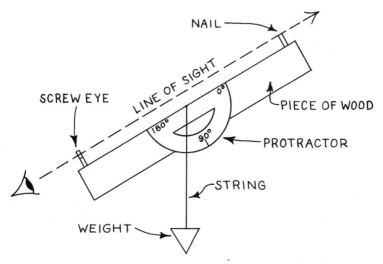

A simple elevation-only tracking device.

number read right off the scale. Trackers such as this one are easy to use and, when properly operated, are surprisingly accurate.

This type of tracking device is for measuring *elevation only*. That is to say, it will only give you the correct altitude if the rocket goes straight up. This will be easier to understand if you know some general trigonometric rules. The figure on page 98 is a right triangle with sides a, b, and c. Side a is the distance from the ignition point to the tracker. Side b is the altitude of the rocket. Now the tangent of angle T multiplied by side a is equal to the altitude. Suppose the distance of side a is 100 meters and at the top of the flight the angle registered by the tracker is 67 degrees. The tangent is, according to the table of tangents in Appendix 2, 2.36. Now 2.36×100 equals 236, but because of the possibility for slight error, round off to the nearest ten units, thus, the altitude is 240 meters.

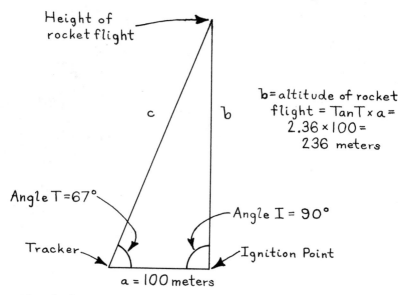

b = altitude of rocket flight = Tan T x a = 2.36 × 100 = 236 meters

Height of rocket flight

c

b

Angle T = 67°

Angle I = 90°

Tracker

Ignition Point

a = 100 meters

Altitude determinations through tangents.

If a model weathercocks into the wind, however, the angle at *I* ceases to be 90 degrees. Then, naturally, none of the trigonometric functions of right angles hold. This may be corrected somewhat by placing the tracker at right angles to any cross wind. In this case, whereas the model may move from left to right, side *b* will be virtually perpendicular.[1]

This type of altitude determination is only accurate within ±10 per cent even with good weather conditions and a skilled operator. Accuracy may be increased a great deal by using more than one tracking device. These should be placed at measured distances from the launcher *in opposite directions*.

[1] For accurate readings, a launch rail or extra stiff launch rod should be used to prevent launcher tip-off, which occurs when thrust bends the launch rod causing the rocket to veer off.

Unlike tracking with a single device where the tracker must be placed at right angles to the prevailing wind, the trackers should always be on a line and *with the wind*. For example, if the wind is blowing towards the west one tracker must be due east of the ignition point and one tracker due west. Actually, the distance of each tracker from the launch point does not matter. One could be 200 meters and one could be 150 meters from it.

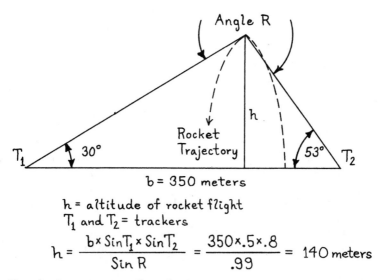

Altitude determinations through sines.

We use tangents when we calculate altitude with one tracker. With two the calculations are different and we use sines. The formula for finding the altitude using the above method is $\dfrac{b \times \sin T_1 \times \sin T_2,}{\sin R}$ referring, of course, to points in the diagram on this page. A simple example will illustrate how this works:

Assume the baseline (b) equal to 350 meters. One tracker (T_1) reports an angle of 30° and the other (T_2) reports an angle of 53°. 53°+30°=83°. Since there are 180° in a triangle, 180°−83°=97° which is angle R. Using the table in Appendix 2 we find the sine of 30°=.5 and the sine of 53°=.8. The sine of any angle greater than 90° equals the sine of 180° minus that angle. Therefore, sine of 97°=sine 83°=.99. Now, substitute into the equation: $\dfrac{350 \times .5 \times .8}{.99}$, or 141. Rounding off to the nearest 10 gives a final altitude of 140 meters.

Tracking devices are easy to build and there are many available as commercial kits. We have designed and built several trackers and, if you are interested, here is the plan for one of the more successful models.

APOGEE MARK V OPTICAL TRACKING UNIT

Materials:

Body tube 30 centimeters (12 inches) long by 5 centimeters (1¼ inches) diameter

Steel, plastic, or paper protractor

A weight (may be 30 grams [1 ounce] paraffin, lead, or any heavy object)

Heavy nylon or cotton shroud line

Plus a knife, modeling cement, fin-spacing guide, and a pencil

This tracking device is a variation of that shown in the diagram on page 97. The basic difference is that the line of sight runs through the body tube, aided by two cross hairs, rather than along the top of a piece of wood.

To make the cross hairs, first turn to the fin placement guide on page 14. Mark an end of the body tube as you would for spacing four fins. Draw four lines from these points back along the body tube for about 4 inches (or 10 centimeters). Next, with your knife cut short slots where the lines intersect the end of the body tube. Take some shroud line, knot one end, and loop it through the slots to form a cross hair. Now, using the marked lines as a guide, cut four additional short slots about 4 inches (or 10 centimeters) from the end of the tube containing the first cross hair. Push shroud line through the slots to form a second cross hair. Glue and/or tie off the ends of the line to hold the cross hairs firmly in place.

The easiest method for installing the protractor is to cement it on the body tube as shown in the diagram on page 97. Be sure the protractor is positioned exactly horizontal with the line of the body tube. If it isn't, your readings will be off.

You need some method of reading the angle of elevation, so here's the final step. Attach, by tying, gluing, or otherwise, the 30-gram (1-ounce) weight to about 30 centimeters (12 inches) of shroud line. Next, cement or tape the other end of the shroud line to the body tube in such a way that the weight pulls the string taut and over the *90-degree* point when the tracker is perfectly horizontal. Except for paint or decals, the Apogee Mark V Optical Tracking Unit is ready for use.

To operate, simply follow the rocket to its peak altitude by looking through the body tube and then hold steady while another person reads the angle of elevation. For accurate results have the two cross hairs coincide on the rocket at the same time.

When two tracking devices are used, each operator should stop tracking the model at the same time. If one tracker stops before or after the other tracker, the altitude calculated will be inaccurate. Therefore, when the puff of the ejection charge is seen, all tracking should stop immediately.

How this tracking device is used should be obvious from the previous discussion. However, unless the tracker and the launcher are on the same plane, a correction factor may be necessary. This involves simply taking any difference between the altitude of the ignition point and the altitude of the tracker and subtracting or adding that difference from the calculated altitude of the rocket.

There is probably little reason why you, as an individual, would require more accuracy than the above system provides. However, if you design primarily contest models or if you desire competition accuracy for club activities, another tracking method is available. This employs trackers that measure not only the elevation angle but also the horizontal, or azimuth, angle. Tracking devices of this nature are called *theodolites*. With this type of setup, you really *do* have to learn trigonometry. So if you're really interested in this super-accurate method of altitude determination consult the starred references on page 125. Theodolites cost as little as $30.00 a pair and are the only tracking instruments approved for use at NAR meets.

In any range it is imperative to have some type of communication system between the people tracking and launch control. The operators obviously need to report their elevation angles for rapid data reduction. They should also be aware of the exact countdown in order to be ready to track. Ideally this would be a land telephone system. Its main advantages are that it enables operators to hear the countdown and also break in in case of a last-minute problem with the tracking device. Unfortunately, these are beyond the budget for all but the most advanced clubs. They also present their own problems. They are hard to set up and are subject to numerous mechanical breakdowns. In addition, unless communication lines are buried, they may present a serious hazard to spectators and recovery crews who have their eyes on the rocket and not on the ground. If you have a permanent launch site and can bury a properly insulated cable without too much difficulty and where the investment of time and money will be worth it,

A highly accurate theodolite.

that's great. Several references in the Selected Readings for this chapter describe such a system in detail. These are the books by Ballah and Gray, Brinley, and Stine.

The communications system we prefer, and have used for several years, consists of four two-channel walkie-talkie citizen's band transceivers. Each transceiver costs about $15.00 including crystals for both channels—which is about the cost of a good phone system. They are portable, need no wires, are fairly simple to have repaired (as opposed to buried cable), and don't have to be permanently installed; therefore they can be used for other purposes between launches.

For best use, each person tracking should have a transceiver; another should go to launch control and the fourth to the emergency officer. The function of the emergency officer, who is stationed at launch control, is to switch on the alternate channel (i.e., the channel not being used for the countdown) and listen for abort calls from the operators. If an operator knocks his tracking device out of alignment, notes a spectator in a restricted area, sees an airplane approaching, or finds anything amiss, he switches to the emergency channel and asks for an abort. The emergency officer then takes appropriate action.

CHAPTER 12

Science fair projects and research

Many local, regional, and national science fairs are held each year. These are naturals for the advanced *and* the novice model rocketeer not only to win awards but also to make contributions to the space sciences as well as model rocketry. A science fair project can range from as simple an exhibit as basic model rocketry to an investigation of the Krushnic Effect.

Carl Guernsey, an eighth-grade student from Camp Hill, Pennsylvania, studied the effects of acceleration on algae. He launched measured samples at different accelerations and studied the results. Using a microscope, Carl discovered the cells *appeared* intact. However, these same cells exhibited retarded growth when cultured.[1]

Several new questions are raised by this experiment. Was the disturbance genetic? Did the rate of growth vary directly with the increased acceleration? More seriously, could this disturbance cause the same or similar reaction in animals such as man? Also, algae is being considered for growth *in flight* on manned interplanetary space flights to provide oxygen and food. Guernsey's experiment could

[1] First Award, Estes Science Fair 1968. *Model Rocket News*, 8 (November, 1968), p. 12.

have grave implications for our astronauts. If the growth of algae is hampered by severe acceleration during take-off, astronauts could starve or suffocate halfway to their destination.

Many rocketeers, although they would like to study some aspect of model rocketry and enter their projects in science fairs, aren't sure how to go about it. This chapter will show you how to develop a scientific investigation and then put it together for an exhibit in any science fair.

A scientific project comprises two parts: research and report. The primary step is to select a topic. This may seem easy, but many rocketeers go astray here and ruin their chances of success. It is important to select a topic that *interests* you. In other words, if you are choosing between a project that turns you on and one you think has a chance to win, pick the project that turns you on. Otherwise, chances are you'll get bored halfway through and drop the whole thing. At least you'll do a good job on something you really want to know.

Then consider your budget. A *budget* includes everything you have available to you. It not only means money but also the recovery area you will use, the capacity of your launcher, and the location of your launch area. If your finances total $10.00, forget investigating the Krushnic Effect. A thrust-time recorder alone can cost over $12.00. If your recovery area is 50 by 100 feet, a project involving boost-gliders, high-altitude probes, or constant payload recovery is out of the question also. Any study involving clustered engines would be foolish if your launcher has a capacity of only 6 or 12 volts. Again, give up a project requiring heavy equipment if the launch site is reachable only after a mile-and-a-half hike. Other considerations may also force an idea to be dropped. In any case, *think out* the project. It's much easier to stop in the beginning than halfway through.

Finally, does your science fair have a theme? If it's biology or medicine, don't investigate aerial photography. If it's aerodynamics, don't try the effects of acceleration on algae.

Make these considerations early. The more time you can spend on the project itself, the better.

Next, form a *hypothesis*—that is, an educated guess on *what* will happen in a given experiment. A *theory*, on the other hand, is an educated guess on *why* something happened in a given experiment. You can prove or disprove both a hypothesis and a theory.

For example, your subject is the Krushnic Effect. You form a hypothesis that when the nozzle of an engine is inserted a certain distance into a body tube, it loses thrust. Experiments are done and the hypothesis is proved.

Now you form a theory: sonic waves from the exhaust "echo" off the sides, muffling the main jet and thereby reduce thrust. Your original hypothesis has been proved; your theory remains just a theory for the present—it may be proved or disproved at some other time with the discovery of new knowledge.

If your hypothesis is contradicted, a theory can still be proposed on why your hypothesis *wasn't* correct. Your study can be a complete success even if your hypothesis is incorrect.

However, look out for misleading results. If you flip a coin once and it comes up heads, you can't theorize that a coin will always come up heads. Right? An experiment has to be repeated many times for accuracy. Also, a single experiment can have results that are way off. Take the following altitudes of a model rocket (same rocket, same type engine, same conditions): 695 feet, 690 feet, 690 feet, 1050 feet. The last altitude reading is due to some error, so throw it out and take the average 690±5 feet.

Once you have your hypothesis, the difficult research

Model rocketry reference books.   *Model Rocketry* magazine.

starts in the *library* (plus technical reports, design manuals, etc., available from model rocket companies and organizations). Find out all you can about your particular subject. This avoids unnecessary repetition of experiments and may suggest new methods to you. Check the special list of references in the Selected Readings. Be sure to write down all the books and articles used (standard form is the one we use in the Selected Readings for each chapter) so you can include them in a bibliography for your report.

Okay. Subject chosen. Hypothesis formed. After you've read and noted all that's necessary, plan your study. Whether you are going to launch plant seedlings under different accelerations or test mathematical formulas in actual practice, the same procedures have to be followed if the results are to be valuable.

First, plan your study so your series of experiments will either prove or disprove your hypothesis. As mentioned before, repeat each experiment. The more tests done, the more precise the results. Flip a coin twice and the odds are not so astronomical that heads will come up both times. After ten tries, you get better accuracy. Flip a coin 10,000 times, and the ratio of heads to tails will be close to the true probability of 50:50.

Assemble your materials and record all equipment, specimens, and so forth in a notebook. You should already have a notebook (see Chapter 2), but it helps to keep a separate one for your project. This notebook doesn't have to be loose-leaf; any sort of spiral- or composition-type will do. The point is: write *everything* down. Take snapshots of each test, especially if you are using biological payloads, and, if you are using a microscope in the experiment, make drawings. Microphotography is better still if you can get an adapter for your microscope.

When the experiments are over, you must then evaluate your results. All your work so far won't be worth a burnt-out engine casing if you can't draw any conclusions! Of course, the main thing is whether your hypothesis was proved or not. Write that down.

Now, why did you get those results? What other experiments could be carried out (not now and not necessarily by you) to support or blow your theory? When you finish that page, your project is complete.

It's time to let the judges and the audience in on it. This is called a *report*. Among scientists this means publishing in a professional journal. To the model rocketeer, it's exhibiting at a science fair or maybe receiving an A in a science class. Anyway, read on to see how to show your project.

Before starting to construct your exhibit, check the rules of the science fair. Many of them prohibit or restrict the handling of bacterial and mold cultures, displays of hypodermic needles, syringes, and the like. There are nearly always special rules for exhibits needing electric current. Then there's the matter of space. For instance, International Science Fair regulations state that an exhibit may not be more than 2½ feet deep and 4 feet wide. Some fairs also limit the height.

Here are a few things to keep in mind:

1. Show-off gimmicks such as rotating lights, etc., which don't add anything to understanding your project, are kid stuff and should be avoided.
2. If your exhibit has any working parts, *make sure they work.*
3. Stick to two or three basic colors. If you need more colors for graphs, etc., use variations on one of the basics (yellow-green, grass green, medium green, dark green). Too many colors make the display seem cluttered. Spectators and judges pass these projects in a hurry.
4. Use lots of enlarged photographs arranged in sequence and with short captions to tell your story effectively. NOTE: Don't—repeat, *don't*—try to show all your experiments. One is enough to give the general scoop on how they were all conducted. Better yet, run either slides or movies. An 8-millimeter loop automatically rewinds and can be shown over and over again without your touching the projector. Loops are made with ordinary, developed 8-millimeter film, and you can have the loop made at a good camera shop. The same effect can be gotten with a circular slide projector. You could even go all out with a sound track or use sound alone to tell your story. For example (and make it short: about 1 minute), a model rocket flight would have checking

procedures, countdown, whoosh of rocket (place mike of tape recorder within 6 inches of launch rod), recovery crews reporting in via walkie-talkie or other means, and finally the report on condition of payload, if any. With your still photos in order, the audience can follow the whole bit and it's a very impressive project.

5. Don't get carried away by fancy construction. The main idea of display is still to report your results and conclusions.

6. Above all, the project should be clear to the average person. Would your kid brother understand it?

As far as actual construction of the display goes (i.e., booth, display case, etc.), here are some references that will help you.

A LISTING OF LIBRARY AND OTHER SPECIAL READINGS AND REFERENCES FOR INFORMATION FOR SCIENCE FAIR PROJECTS

Articles, general magazine (*Reader's Guide to Periodical Literature*)

Articles, newspaper (*New York Times Index*)

Articles, science magazines (special indexes of periodical guide)

Books (look up subject in card catalogue)

Books on related subjects (for example, for information on how to grow seedlings, look through all Dewey decimal number 580s [Botany] on the shelves, as well as just books on laboratory techniques for growing plants)

General encyclopedias

Science or specific encyclopedias

Look up exact subject and *related* subjects. For instance, don't just look up "rocket." Cross references for "rocket" are:

Air
Airplane
Ammunition
Artillery
Aviation
Bazooka
Congreve, Sir William
Fireworks
Goddard, Robert H.
Guided missile
Invention (inventions of the future)
Jato
Jet propulsion
Signaling
Space travel
Telemetry
Yeager, Charles

To this could be added *aerodynamics, astronautics, acceleration, gravity, drag, friction,* etc.

Magazines, newsletters, and books specifically on model rocketry are not exactly plentiful, but we list some in the Selected Readings and Appendix 1 at the end of the book.

For current articles in general magazines, see the *Reader's Guide to Periodical Literature* under *ROCKETS—Models* or *ROCKETS—Amateur experiments.*

Teachers, parents, and friends can give you ideas too. A lot depends on what kind of props the fair provides. You may have to build your own booth, carry in your own card table, or make your own display case.

Let's suppose you have to build your own booth. This

can consist of merely three sections of plywood, pegboard, or Artboard hinged together. The advantage for you here is being able to fold it up and carry it in and out easily.

On a table in front of your booth you should have a brief written report of your experiments and results as well as any models, projectors, etc.

There are several books on science fairs. Ask your librarian and also look around Dewey decimal number 507.2 on the open shelves. If you have a chance to visit another science fair first, do so, and be prepared to take notes. You'll see immediately why some projects look professional and others amateurish.

It's easy to move up from the school, local, and regional science fair level. Some of the model rocket companies listed in Appendix 1 offer monthly awards to model rocketeers for research and development of new and better model rocket systems and designs. Others give prizes for the best projects having to do with model rocketry entered in science fairs throughout the country.

Also, at the National Association of Rocketry's National Meet every year, an R & D (Research and Development) contest is held. Anyone who is an NAR member at the time and is able to attend may enter a project. Many small clubs and chartered sections hold their own contests too. Add to this the fact that many small science fairs send finalists to higher-level fairs that may lead to their winning scholarships and grants; a good project can be quite profitable.

Most projects never reach fame or fortune, however. Strangely enough, most rocketeers enter contests simply for fun.

Hitting your friends
with a club

Are you ready for a wind tunnel, a centrifuge, or a complete
rocket range with heavy-duty launchers and launch panels?
Are you independently wealthy? If the answer is "yes"
to the first but "no" to the second, there is a solution to
the problem—a club, or, as the masses put it, a model
rocket research society.

Whatever you call it, a club has advantages for both
the new and the experienced model rocketeer. If there's
one currently operating at your school or in your town,
join it. If there isn't, round up some friends and start one.

There are two types of clubs: the casual type, which
is good for small groups of rocketeers, and the organization
type, best for groups of fifteen or more.

The small club is just an informal kind of thing. You
and your buddies get together for launches and discussions.
Each member pitches in by buying or helping to buy
certain equipment which is then used by everyone. This
doesn't mean you can't have a president—in fact, you'll
need one to plan launches, keep an inventory of and find
a storage place for the club equipment, and even hold an
occasional meeting.

It's a good idea to bring in an adult sponsor since the

community is more likely to recognize the club if you have adult supervision. You can also look for an organization to sponsor the club, such as a service club or the town recreation department. The first place to try, though, is the science department of your school. A school affiliation has many advantages, not the least of which is that science teachers are natural-born scroungers and always seem to know just where to find the scrap you need to build, say, a wind tunnel.

You may be faced with resistance when you first confront a group of adults because they do not understand what you mean when you use the word "rocketry." They will probably bring up the case of a boy who blew off his hand while building a rocket. When you talk to an organization you should start off by explaining the difference between the model rocketeer and the "basement bomber." Make it clear that the boy would not have been injured had he used model rockets and commercial engines instead of metal pipe and home-brew propellant.

It sounds dull to start off with rules and regulations, but when you have fifteen or more people all clowning around, you don't accomplish much. Your club will need a president, secretary-treasurer, and sergeant-at-arms if nothing else. The sergeant-at-arms keeps order, and all of you together better decide what that means. In other words, some kids may have to be expelled for misconduct, and it's best to be ready for it in advance. Anyone who starts making his own fuel gets thrown out immediately.

At your first meeting be prepared to decide upon things like dues, committees (temporary), and general procedure. Oh yes, don't forget to decide on the time, place, and date for your *next* meeting. Think about writing a simple constitution. It can always be amended if it doesn't work out the way you thought it would. Just so you get it down and agreed upon.

As the club membership grows, you'll need standing committees, each with a leader. For example, a supply committee can order for all members of the club at one time and often get a discount. One committee can be in charge of the range operations. Another could work out the details of a rocket contest. Members can belong to several committees at once, of course.

Eventually you may vote to become an official section of the National Association of Rocketry or, if your club is affiliated with a school or youth organization, joining Space Clubs of America. Both of these have club insurance and send materials to clubs. Write to these two organizations and see whether it's worth while to affiliate.

Probably one of your first club projects will be a rocket contest. Members can compete in the height their birds go (altitude), the length of time they are in the air (duration), scale, and design. In altitude events it is necessary to have a very accurate tracking and altitude-computing system. In duration tests the rocket is timed from ignition to touch down. There are two types of duration events: boost-glider and parachute. The boost-glider must ascend vertically under power and descend in a glide. In parachute duration contests, it must be decided whether a semiparachute or regular parachute will be used. Scale events test the rockets for their likeness to the real thing, their workmanship, and how well they fly. In design contests rockets are judged for originality, flight characteristics, and general good looks.

When you hold a contest, certain rules are upheld and certain equipment used. All contests in which *national contest points* are desired by the entrants must be sanctioned by the NAR Contest Board. For this sanction, apply to the NAR (CAR for Canadians). All contests by U.S. model rocketeers are conducted under the United States Model Rocket Sporting Code.

Research equipment is not difficult to make and helps everyone improve their rocketry. You can make a device to measure thrust by using a kitchen scale or any small scale that does not involve balancing. The engine tested should be attached to a large board. The board is put on top of the scale and its weight noted. When the engine is ignited, its thrust will push down the scale showing the measurable force.

A centrifuge can be constructed for testing payloads by using part of a bicycle. The bike is turned upside down, and you use the back wheel. A compartment for the payload is built on the inner part of the wheel, and you just work the pedals to turn the wheel.

A wind tunnel is used to test how stable the rocket is by the way it points into the wind. A simple wind tunnel can be built out of wood, many engine mailing and body tubes, clear plastic, and an electric fan. Make a box about 2 feet (.6 meters) square, open at opposite ends, out of the wood. Inside this box glue the tubes with open ends corresponding with the ends of the box. At one end of the box fit the electric fan so it will blow into the box and through the tubes. The junction between fan and box should be sealed so no air gets out around the edges. At the other end of the box make a little compartment out of clear plastic so the wind, after passing through the mailing tubes, can go through the plastic compartment and out. Tie a thread to your rocket at the CG and hang it inside the plastic compartment. Then you can observe the rocket's reactions.

A club can set up a model rocket library. Some of the dues can go for books and subscriptions to various magazines: *American Modeler, NASA Facts, Model Rocketry, Model Rocket News, American Rocketeer,* and others. The library can also keep a notebook of club records and model rocket flight data.

In addition to being able to order supplies and equipment from model rocket companies in large amounts and, therefore, at a discount, clubs are also sent free information on request. The club secretary should write every model rocket company and ask to be put on the mailing list as a club.

There are great advantages to belonging to a club, and it's worth the time and effort it takes to get everything organized. But plan it well. One we belonged to folded after six haphazard months of rapidly dwindling interest, not in model rocketry but in meetings. With good ideas and plans, however, you'll have fun and probably learn more than you could alone.

CHAPTER 14

From kits to computers

Model rocketry is not static. What got you into model rocketry was probably the same emotion that made sky-rockets popular more than 1000 years ago. Perhaps you'll be held by the same sense of accomplishment a model aircraft enthusiast gets out of his hobby. Most likely, though, you'll find your interest in model rocketry continues because it is completely relevant to today's aerospace technology. The opportunities for research and progress are endless.

Many model rocketeers are college students, and one of the most advanced model rocket clubs in the United States is the M.I.T. Model Rocket Society at the Massachusetts Institute of Technology, Cambridge, Massachusetts. At one model rocket convention, papers were presented on topics such as the "Aerodynamic Force Effects on Model Rocket Motion."[1] There is also an active club at Purdue University.

Model rocketry can even help you get into college. Ron J. Lagoe of Oswego, New York, received a $5000 scholarship from Hughes Aircraft for a scale "Surveyor" he built. This was a touch more ambitious than it seems because

[1] By Gordon Mandell, then an M.I.T. junior, majoring in aeronautics and astronautics. This is a bit more technical than you're probably inclined right now.

the principle involved was *retrorockets*. The model was dropped 83 feet (26 meters) and braked successfully for a soft landing five times. In addition to one main (braking) *retro* engine, three smaller guidance, or *vernier*, rockets were also ignited. On the sixth flight, unfortunately, one of the verniers failed and the model crashed.

Model rocketry has received increasing attention, whether to the safe delivery of an egg sent into space by a junior high science class and reported on the local news or the launching of a scale model Saturn V during the half time of a Bowl Game in the Astrodome. Restrictive laws are rapidly disappearing, thanks to the work of many rocketeers. In Massachusetts, Gary Townsend, age seventeen, personally pushed through the legislature the law exempting model rocketry from the old fireworks codes.

Somewhere between the kit and the computer, a casual hobby has turned into a serious endeavor and even an occupation. Internationally, the old political lines that kept East and West apart are non-existent in model rocketry. International competitions are bringing together students and specialists whose interests transcend ideologies, a sort of balsa-and-paper Olympics.

All we are saying is that there's more to model rocketry than the excitement of pushing your first launch button. Model rocketry is a dynamic part of the Space Age and so are you.

Selected Readings

CHAPTER 1

Herrik, John W., and others, eds. *Rocket Encyclopedia Illustrated.* Los Angeles: Aero Publishers, Inc., 1959.

Matson, Wayne R. *Educators Guide to Model Rocketry.* Phoenix, Arizona: Centuri Engineering Co., 1968.

"A Rocketeer's Guide to Avoid Suicide." Penrose, Colorado: Estes Industries, Inc., 1964.

Staffel, Joseph F. "Basement Bombers—A Fire-Police Responsibility," *Police,* November–December, 1965. Reprinted by Estes Industries, Inc.

Why Model Rocketry? Penrose, Colorado: Estes Industries, Inc., 1964.

CHAPTER 2

Black, Dean. "Fins," *Model Rocket News.* (Penrose, Colorado: Estes Industries, Inc.), 3, April–May, 1963.

"Build It Right . . . the First Time!" *Model Rocket News,* 4, November, 1964.

"Model Finishing," *Model Rocket News,* 6, April, 1966.

Model Rocketry—The Educational Space-Age Hobby. Penrose, Colorado: Estes Industries, Inc., 1966.

National Association of Rocketry Staff. *Basic Model Rocketry* (NAR Technical Report ⚹9). McLean, Virginia: National Association of Rocketry.

Roe, William S. *Rolling Body Tubes* (NAR Technical Report ⚹10). McLean, Virginia: National Association of Rocketry.

Stine, G. Harry. *Handbook of Model Rocketry,* 2nd ed. Chicago: Follett Publishing Co., 1967. Chap. 2.

Stine, G. Harry. "Model Rocketry Goes Metric," *American Modeler Magazine,* March, 1968.

Tydings, Rick, Jr. *Turning Balsa Nose Cones on ¼" Electric Drills* (NAR Technical Report ⚹6). McLean, Virginia: National Association of Rocketry.

CHAPTER 3

Ballistics Manual for the Model Rocketeer, Sec. II–*Internal Ballistics.* Seymour, Indiana: Rocket Development Corporation, 1966.

Estes, Vernon. *Youth Rocket Safety* (A Report to the Model Rocket Manufacturers Association). Penrose, Colorado: Estes Industries, Inc., 1967.

"The Liquid Fueled Vashon 'Valkyrie 2.'" *Flying Models Magazine,* 380, November, 1968, 28, 34–35.

National Aeronautics and Space Administration, *Rocket Propulsion* (NASA Facts). Washington, D.C.: U. S. Government Printing Office, 0–281–835.

Stine, G. Harry. *Handbook of Model Rocketry,* 2nd ed. Chicago: Follett Publishing Co., 1967. Chap. 3.

Plus the manufacturers' catalogues.

CHAPTER 4

Contest Range (NAR Plan Program Fact Sheet ⅙401). McLean, Virginia: National Association of Rocketry.

"Launching Systems." *Model Rocket News.* (Penrose, Colorado: Estes Industries, Inc.), 5, December, 1965, 1–2.

National Aeronautics and Space Administration. *The Countdown* (NASA Facts). Washington, D.C.: U. S. Government Printing Office, 0–269–949.

Reliable Cluster Ignition (Centuri Engineering Technical Information Report TIR–52). Phoenix, Arizona: Centuri Engineering Co., 1968.

Roe, John S., and William S. Roe, and G. Harry Stine. *Building a Range Firing Panel and Communications System* (NAR Technical Report ⅙2). McLean, Virginia: National Association of Rocketry.

Stine, G. Harry. *Handbook of Model Rocketry,* 2nd ed. Chicago: Follett Publishing Co., 1967. Chaps. 4 and 13.

Toal, David. "The Orange and Black (An Underwater Rocket)," *Model Rocket News* (*The Best From Volumes One and Two*), 6.

U.S. Model Rocket Sporting Code (1967 ed.). Washington, D.C.: National Association of Rocketry, 1967. Sect. 5.

CHAPTER 9

Abbot, I. H., and A. E. Von Doenhoff. *Theory of Wing Sections.* New York: Dover Publications, Inc., 1959.

Malewicki, Douglas J. "The Radio Controlled Boost/Glider," *Model Rocketry Magazine,* 1, August, 1969, 5–9.

Mandell, Gordon. *Front Engine Boost-Gliders* (Estes Industries Technical Report ₩TR-7). Penrose, Colorado: Estes Industries, Inc., 1964.

Mandell, Gordon. *Rear-Engine Boost-Gliders* (Estes Industries Technical Report ₩TR-4). Penrose, Colorado: Estes Industries, Inc., 1963.

Renger, Larry. "Pop Pod," *Model Rocket News* (Penrose, Colorado: Estes Industries, Inc.), 5, December, 1965, 6.

Stine, G. Harry. *Handbook of Model Rocketry,* 2nd ed. Chicago: Follett Publishing Co., 1967. Chap. 9.

Zaic, Frank. *Circular Airflow and Model Aircraft.* Northridge, California: Model Aeronautic Publications, 1964.

CHAPTER 11

"Altitude Calculations Made Simple!" *Model Rocket News* (Penrose Colorado: Estes Industries, Inc.), 6, April, 1966, 5–6.

*Ballah, Arthur and Grant A. Gray. *Project Eyeball: An Optical Tracking System* (NAR Technical Report ₩3). McLean, Virginia: National Association of Rocketry.

*Brinley, Capt. Bertrand R. *Rocket Manual for Amateurs.* New York: Ballantine Books, Inc., 1960. Chap. 10.

Estes Industries, Inc. *Altitude Tracking* (Estes Industries Technical Report TR-3). Penrose, Colorado: Estes Industries, Inc., 1963.

Malewicki, Douglas J. *Model Rocket Altitude Performance* (Centuri Engineering Technical Information Report TIR-100). Phoenix, Arizona: Centuri Engineering Co., 1968.

Malewicki, Douglas J. *Model Rocket Altitude Prediction Charts Including Aerodynamic Drag* (Estes Industries Technical Report TR-10), Penrose, Colorado: Estes Industries, Inc., 1967.

Stine, G. Harry. "Countdown," *American Aircraft Modeler* 66, July, 1968, 38.

* Stine, G. Harry. *Handbook of Model Rocketry,* 2nd ed. Chicago: Follett Publishing Company, 1967. Chap. 12.

CHAPTER 12

Beveridge, W. I. B. *The Art of Scientific Investigation*, 3rd ed. New York: Vintage Books, 1957.

"Developing a Winning Science Fair Project." *Model Rocket News*, (Penrose, Colorado: Estes Industries, Inc.), 3, August–September, 1963, 1–3.

"Estes Science Fair Contest Winners!" *Model Rocket News*, 8, November, 1968, 12.

"Model Rocketry and the Science Fair." *Model Rocket News*, 3, February–March, 1963, 1, 10–12.

National Association of Rocketry Publications Committee. *R & D Methods Guide*. McLean, Virginia: National Association of Rocketry, 1968.

Sawyer, R. W. and R. A. Farmer. *New Ideas for Science Fair Projects*. New York: Arco Publishing Co., Inc., 1967.

"Schmidt Project Named Best in Science Fair Contest." *Model Rocket News*, 3, August–September, 1963, 1–2.

"Science Fair Results." *Model Rocket News*, 6, December, 1966, 1–2.

CHAPTER 13

Canadian Association of Rocketry. *Model Rocketry in Canada*. Ottawa, Ontario: Canadian Association of Rocketry, 1967.

Estes Industries, Inc. *Guide for Rocket Clubs*. Penrose, Colorado: Estes Industries, Inc.,

Matson, Wayne R. *Educators' Guide to Model Rocketry*. Phoenix, Arizona: Centuri Engineering Co., 1968.

National Association of Rocketry. *Preliminary Contest Procedures* (NAR Technical Report #101–104). McLean, Virginia: National Association of Rocketry.

National Association of Rocketry. *Section Organization Guide and Application*. McLean, Virginia: National Association of Rocketry.

National Association of Rocketry. *U.S. Model Rocket Sporting Code*. McLean, Virginia: National Association of Rocketry, 1967.

Stine, G. Harry. *Handbook of Model Rocketry*, 2nd ed. Chicago: Follett Publishing Co., 1967. Chap. 14.

Appendix 1

MODEL ROCKET COMPANIES

CENTURI ENGINEERING COMPANY, INC. P. O. Box 1988, Phoenix, Arizona 85001
   Kits, engines, technical reports, cluster rockets, multistage rockets, B/Gs, D–F engines, D–F kits, launcher kits, newsletter.
COMPETITION MODEL ROCKETS. P. O. Box 7022, Alexandria, Virginia 22307
   Kits, cluster rockets, multistage rockets, B/Gs.
ESTES INDUSTRIES, INC. P. O. Box 227, Penrose, Colorado 81240
   Kits, engines, technical reports, cluster rockets, multistage rockets, B/Gs, launcher kits, newsletter.
FLIGHT SYSTEMS, INC. P. O. Box 145, Louisville, Colorado 80027
   Kits, engines, cluster rockets, multistage rockets, D–F engines, D–F kits, launcher kits.
SPACE AGE INDUSTRIES. 714 Raritan Avenue, Highland Park, New Jersey 08904
   Kits, B/Gs, D–F kits, launcher kits.
VASHON INDUSTRIES, INC. P. O. Box 309, Vashon, Washington 98070
   Kits, engines, technical reports, launcher kits, liquid fuel.

MODEL ROCKET PUBLICATIONS

American Rocketeer (Centuri Engineering Company) P. O. Box 1988, Phoenix, Arizona 85001
Model Rocket News (Estes Industries, Inc.) P. O. Box 227, Penrose, Colorado 81240
Model Rocketry P. O. Box 214, Astor Station, Boston, Massachusetts 02123

MODEL ROCKET ORGANIZATIONS

Canadian Association of Rocketry
   C/o Royal Canadian Flying Clubs Association
   Suite 207
   2277 Riverside Drive E.
   Ottawa 8, Ontario
   (use complete address)

National Association of Rocketry
 P. O. Box 178
 McLean, Virginia 22101

Space Clubs of America
 P. O. Box 1822
 Newport Beach, California 92663
 (enclose a stamped self-addressed envelope for correspondence)

Appendix 2   Useful Tables

TABLE 1.   Sines, Cosines, and Tangents
(for angles of 0 to 90 degrees)

Degrees of Angle	Sin	Tan	Degrees of Angle	Sin	Tan	Degrees of Angle	Sin	Tan
0	0.000	0.000	31	0.515	0.601	61	0.875	1.804
1	0.017	0.018	32	0.530	0.625	62	0.883	1.881
2	0.035	0.035	33	0.545	0.649	63	0.891	1.963
3	0.052	0.052	34	0.559	0.675	64	0.899	2.050
4	0.070	0.070	35	0.574	0.700	65	0.906	2.145
5	0.087	0.088						
6	0.105	0.105	36	0.588	0.727	66	0.914	2.246
7	0.122	0.123	37	0.602	0.754	67	0.921	2.356
8	0.139	0.141	38	0.616	0.781	68	0.927	2.457
9	0.156	0.158	39	0.629	0.810	69	0.934	2.605
10	0.174	0.176	40	0.643	0.839	70	0.940	2.747
11	0.191	0.194	41	0.656	0.869	71	0.946	2.904
12	0.208	0.213	42	0.669	0.900	72	0.951	3.078
13	0.225	0.231	43	0.682	0.933	73	0.956	3.271
14	0.242	0.249	44	0.695	0.966	74	0.961	3.487
15	0.259	0.268	45	0.707	1.000	75	0.966	3.732
16	0.276	0.287	46	0.719	1.036	76	0.970	4.011
17	0.292	0.306	47	0.731	1.072	77	0.974	4.331
18	0.309	0.325	48	0.743	1.111	78	0.978	4.705
19	0.326	0.344	49	0.755	1.150	79	0.982	5.145
20	0.342	0.364	50	0.766	1.192	80	0.985	5.671
21	0.358	0.384	51	0.777	1.235	81	0.988	6.314
22	0.375	0.404	52	0.788	1.280	82	0.990	7.115
23	0.391	0.425	53	0.799	1.327	83	0.993	8.144
24	0.407	0.445	54	0.809	1.376	84	0.995	9.514
25	0.423	0.466	55	0.819	1.428	85	0.996	11.43
26	0.438	0.488	56	0.829	1.483	86	0.998	14.30
27	0.454	0.510	57	0.839	1.540	87	0.999	19.80
28	0.470	0.532	58	0.848	1.600	88	0.999	28.64
29	0.485	0.554	59	0.875	1.664	89	1.000	57.29
30	0.500	0.577	60	0.866	1.732	90	1.000	—

Cosine values can be found as follows:
Cos of angle = sin (90 degrees − angle)

TABLE 2. Natural, or Napierian, Logarithms
(for values, N, from 1.00 to 9.99)

To find the natural log of a number that is 1/10, 1/100, 1/1000, etc., of a number whose log is given, subtract from the given logarithm $\log_e$ 10, 2 $\log_e$ 10, 3 $\log_e$ 10, etc. To find the natural log of a number that is 10, 100, 1000, etc., times a number whose log is given, add to the given logarithm $\log_e$ 10, 2 $\log_e$ 10, 3 $\log_e$ 10, etc.

$$\log_e 10 = 2.30 \qquad 6\log_e 10 = 13.82$$
$$2\log_e 10 = 4.61 \qquad 7\log_e 10 = 16.12$$
$$3\log_e 10 = 6.91 \qquad 8\log_e 10 = 18.42$$
$$4\log_e 10 = 9.21 \qquad 9\log_e 10 = 20.72$$
$$5\log_e 10 = 11.51 \qquad 10\log_e 10 = 23.03$$

N	.00	.01	.02	.03	.04	.05	.06	.07	.08	.09
1.0	.00	.01	.02	.03	.04	.05	.06	.07	.08	.09
1.1	.09	.10	.11	.12	.13	.14	.15	.16	.17	.17
1.2	.18	.19	.20	.21	.22	.22	.23	.24	.25	.25
1.3	.26	.27	.28	.29	.29	.30	.31	.31	.32	.33
1.4	.34	.34	.35	.36	.36	.37	.38	.39	.39	.40
1.5	.41	.41	.42	.43	.43	.44	.44	.45	.46	.46
1.6	.47	.48	.48	.49	.49	.50	.51	.51	.52	.52
1.7	.53	.54	.54	.55	.55	.56	.56	.57	.58	.58
1.8	.59	.59	.60	.60	.61	.62	.62	.63	.63	.64
1.9	.64	.65	.65	.66	.66	.67	.67	.68	.68	.69
2.0	.69	.70	.70	.71	.71	.72	.72	.73	.73	.74
2.1	.74	.75	.75	.76	.76	.77	.77	.77	.78	.78
2.2	.79	.79	.80	.80	.81	.81	.82	.82	.82	.83
2.3	.83	.84	.84	.85	.85	.85	.86	.86	.87	.87
2.4	.88	.88	.88	.89	.89	.90	.90	.90	.91	.91
2.5	.92	.92	.92	.93	.93	.93	.94	.94	.95	.95
2.6	.96	.96	.96	.97	.97	.97	.98	.98	.99	.99
2.7	.99	1.00	1.00	1.00	1.01	1.01	1.02	1.02	1.02	1.03
2.8	1.03	1.03	1.04	1.04	1.04	1.05	1.05	1.05	1.06	1.06
2.9	1.06	1.07	1.07	1.07	1.08	1.08	1.09	1.09	1.09	1.10
3.0	1.10	1.10	1.11	1.11	1.11	1.12	1.12	1.12	1.12	1.13
3.1	1.13	1.13	1.14	1.14	1.14	1.15	1.15	1.15	1.16	1.16
3.2	1.16	1.17	1.17	1.17	1.18	1.18	1.18	1.18	1.19	1.19
3.3	1.19	1.20	1.20	1.20	1.21	1.21	1.21	1.21	1.22	1.22
3.4	1.22	1.23	1.23	1.23	1.24	1.24	1.24	1.24	1.25	1.25
3.5	1.25	1.26	1.26	1.26	1.26	1.27	1.27	1.27	1.28	1.28
3.6	1.28	1.28	1.29	1.29	1.29	1.29	1.30	1.30	1.30	1.31
3.7	1.31	1.31	1.31	1.32	1.32	1.32	1.32	1.33	1.33	1.33
3.8	1.33	1.34	1.34	1.34	1.35	1.35	1.35	1.35	1.36	1.36
3.9	1.36	1.36	1.37	1.37	1.37	1.37	1.38	1.38	1.38	1.38

TABLE 2. Natural, or Napierian, Logarithms (continued)

N	.00	.01	.02	.03	.04	.05	.06	.07	.08	.09
4.0	1.39	1.39	1.39	1.39	1.40	1.40	1.40	1.40	1.41	1.41
4.1	1.41	1.41	1.42	1.42	1.42	1.42	1.43	1.43	1.43	1.43
4.2	1.44	1.44	1.44	1.44	1.44	1.45	1.45	1.45	1.45	1.46
4.3	1.46	1.46	1.46	1.47	1.47	1.47	1.47	1.47	1.48	1.48
4.4	1.48	1.48	1.49	1.49	1.49	1.49	1.50	1.50	1.50	1.50
4.5	1.50	1.51	1.51	1.51	1.51	1.52	1.52	1.52	1.52	1.52
4.6	1.53	1.53	1.53	1.53	1.53	1.54	1.54	1.54	1.54	1.55
4.7	1.55	1.55	1.55	1.55	1.56	1.56	1.56	1.56	1.56	1.57
4.8	1.57	1.57	1.57	1.57	1.58	1.58	1.58	1.58	1.59	1.59
4.9	1.59	1.59	1.59	1.60	1.60	1.60	1.60	1.60	1.61	1.61
5.0	1.61	1.61	1.61	1.62	1.62	1.62	1.62	1.62	1.63	1.63
5.1	1.63	1.63	1.63	1.64	1.64	1.64	1.64	1.64	1.64	1.65
5.2	1.65	1.65	1.65	1.65	1.66	1.66	1.66	1.66	1.66	1.67
5.3	1.67	1.67	1.67	1.67	1.68	1.68	1.68	1.68	1.68	1.68
5.4	1.69	1.69	1.69	1.69	1.69	1.70	1.70	1.70	1.70	1.70
5.5	1.70	1.71	1.71	1.71	1.71	1.71	1.72	1.72	1.72	1.72
5.6	1.72	1.72	1.73	1.73	1.73	1.73	1.73	1.74	1.74	1.74
5.7	1.74	1.74	1.74	1.75	1.75	1.75	1.75	1.75	1.75	1.76
5.8	1.76	1.76	1.76	1.76	1.76	1.77	1.77	1.77	1.77	1.77
5.9	1.77	1.78	1.78	1.78	1.78	1.78	1.79	1.79	1.79	1.79
6.0	1.79	1.79	1.80	1.80	1.80	1.80	1.80	1.80	1.80	1.81
6.1	1.81	1.81	1.81	1.81	1.81	1.82	1.82	1.82	1.82	1.82
6.2	1.82	1.83	1.83	1.83	1.83	1.83	1.83	1.84	1.84	1.84
6.3	1.84	1.84	1.84	1.85	1.85	1.85	1.85	1.85	1.85	1.85
6.4	1.86	1.86	1.86	1.86	1.86	1.86	1.87	1.87	1.87	1.87
6.5	1.87	1.87	1.87	1.88	1.88	1.88	1.88	1.88	1.88	1.89
6.6	1.89	1.89	1.89	1.89	1.89	1.89	1.90	1.90	1.90	1.90
6.7	1.90	1.89	1.91	1.91	1.91	1.91	1.91	1.91	1.91	1.92
6.8	1.92	1.90	1.92	1.92	1.92	1.92	1.93	1.93	1.93	1.93
6.9	1.93	1.93	1.93	1.94	1.94	1.94	1.94	1.94	1.94	1.94

TABLE 2.   Natural, or Napierian, Logarithms (continued)

N	.00	.01	.02	.03	.04	.05	.06	.07	.08	.09
7.0	1.95	1.95	1.95	1.95	1.95	1.95	1.95	1.96	1.96	1.96
7.1	1.96	1.96	1.96	1.96	1.97	1.97	1.97	1.97	1.97	1.97
7.2	1.97	1.98	1.98	1.98	1.98	1.98	1.98	1.98	1.99	1.99
7.3	1.99	1.99	1.99	1.99	1.99	1.99	2.00	2.00	2.00	2.00
7.4	2.00	2.00	2.00	2.01	2.01	2.01	2.01	2.01	2.01	2.01
7.5	2.01	2.02	2.02	2.02	2.02	2.02	2.02	2.02	2.03	2.03
7.6	2.03	2.03	2.03	2.03	2.03	2.03	2.04	2.04	2.04	2.04
7.7	2.04	2.04	2.04	2.05	2.05	2.05	2.05	2.05	2.05	2.05
7.8	2.05	2.06	2.06	2.06	2.06	2.06	2.06	2.06	2.06	2.07
7.9	2.07	2.07	2.07	2.07	2.07	2.07	2.07	2.08	2.08	2.08
8.0	2.08	2.08	2.08	2.08	2.08	2.09	2.09	2.09	2.09	2.09
8.1	2.09	2.09	2.09	2.10	2.10	2.10	2.10	2.10	2.10	2.10
8.2	2.10	2.11	2.11	2.11	2.11	2.11	2.11	2.11	2.11	2.12
8.3	2.12	2.12	2.12	2.12	2.12	2.12	2.12	2.12	2.13	2.13
8.4	2.13	2.13	2.13	2.13	2.13	2.13	2.14	2.14	2.14	2.14
8.5	2.14	2.14	2.14	2.14	2.14	2.15	2.15	2.15	2.15	2.15
8.6	2.15	2.15	2.15	2.16	2.16	2.16	2.16	2.16	2.16	2.16
8.7	2.16	2.16	2.17	2.17	2.17	2.17	2.17	2.17	2.17	2.17
8.8	2.17	2.18	2.18	2.18	2.18	2.18	2.18	2.18	2.18	2.18
8.9	2.19	2.19	2.19	2.19	2.19	2.19	2.19	2.19	2.19	2.20
9.0	2.20	2.20	2.20	2.20	2.20	2.20	2.20	2.20	2.21	2.21
9.1	2.21	2.21	2.21	2.21	2.21	2.21	2.21	2.22	2.22	2.22
9.2	2.22	2.22	2.22	2.22	2.22	2.22	2.23	2.23	2.23	2.23
9.3	2.23	2.23	2.23	2.23	2.23	2.24	2.24	2.24	2.24	2.24
9.4	2.24	2.24	2.24	2.24	2.24	2.25	2.25	2.25	2.25	2.25
9.5	2.25	2.25	2.25	2.25	2.26	2.26	2.26	2.26	2.26	2.26
9.6	2.26	2.26	2.26	2.26	2.27	2.27	2.27	2.27	2.27	2.27
9.7	2.27	2.27	2.27	2.28	2.28	2.28	2.28	2.28	2.28	2.28
9.8	2.28	2.28	2.28	2.29	2.29	2.29	2.29	2.29	2.29	2.29
9.9	2.29	2.29	2.29	2.30	2.30	2.30	2.30	2.30	2.30	2.30

TABLE 3.   Hyperbolic Functions
(for values, N, from .00 to 10.0)

Note: arc hyperbolic tangent = $\tanh^{-1} \dfrac{1}{\tanh}$

N	Sinh	Cosh	Tanh	N	Sinh	Cosh	Tanh
.00	.00	1.00	.00	2.00	3.63	3.76	.96
.05	.05	1.00	.05	2.05	3.82	3.95	.97
.10	.10	1.00	.10	2.10	4.02	4.14	.97
.15	.15	1.01	.15	2.15	4.23	4.35	.97
.20	.20	1.02	.20	2.20	4.46	4.57	.98
.25	.25	1.03	.25	2.25	4.69	4.80	.98
.30	.30	1.05	.29	2.30	4.94	5.04	.98
.35	.36	1.06	.37	2.35	5.20	5.29	.98
.40	.41	1.08	.38	2.40	5.47	5.56	.98
.45	.47	1.10	.42	2.45	5.75	5.84	.99
.50	.52	1.13	.46	2.50	6.05	6.13	.99
.55	.58	1.16	.50	2.55	6.36	6.44	.99
.60	.64	1.19	.54	2.60	6.69	6.77	.99
.65	.70	1.22	.57	2.65	7.04	7.11	.99
.70	.76	1.26	.60	2.70	7.41	7.47	.99
.75	.82	1.29	.64	2.75	7.79	7.85	.99
.80	.89	1.34	.66	2.80	8.19	8.25	.99
.85	.96	1.38	.69	2.85	8.61	8.67	.99
.90	1.03	1.43	.72	2.90	9.06	9.11	.99
.95	1.10	1.49	.74	2.95	9.53	9.58	.99
1.00	1.18	1.54	.76				
1.05	1.25	1.60	.78				
1.10	1.34	1.67	.80				
1.15	1.42	1.74	.82				
1.20	1.51	1.81	.83	3.0	10.02	10.07	1.00
				3.5	16.54	16.57	1.00
1.25	1.60	1.89	.85				
1.30	1.70	1.97	.86	4.0	27.29	27.31	1.00
1.35	1.80	2.06	.87	4.5	45.00	45.01	1.00
1.40	1.90	2.15	.88	5.0	74.20	74.21	1.00
1.45	2.01	2.25	.90	5.5	122.34	122.35	1.00
1.50	2.13	2.35	.91	6.0	201.71	201.72	1.00
1.55	2.25	2.46	.91	6.5	332.57	332.57	1.00
1.60	2.38	2.58	.92	7.0	548.32	548.32	1.00
1.65	2.51	2.70	.93	7.5	904.02	904.02	1.00
1.70	2.65	2.83	.94				
1.75	2.79	2.96	.94	8.0	1490.5	1490.5	1.00
1.80	2.94	3.11	.95	8.5	2457.4	2457.4	1.00
1.85	3.10	3.26	.95	9.0	4051.5	4051.5	1.00
1.90	3.27	3.42	.96	9.5	6679.9	6679.9	1.00
1.95	3.44	3.59	.96	10.0	11013.2	11013.2	1.00

Appendix 3   Performance Tabulations

The following eight tables were computed
by David Moon, Wayland, Massachusetts.

Key to Symbols

CD	drag coefficient
C.TIME	coast time
G's	measure of acceleration (see Chapter 5)
ACC	acceleration
ALT	altitude
NAR	National Association of Rocketry engine classifications (see Chapter 3)
EJ ALT	altitude of the rocket when ejection charge fires
$/FT-ALT	the average cost of the particular engine divided by the maximum altitude of the rocket; the lower the figure the greater the economy. Note: $-03 = 10^{-3}$ and 10^{-3} is less than 10^{-2} Therefore, $2.61-03 is more economical than $1.01-02
RWT	total rocket weight (in oz. not including engine)
RNE	number of engines (greater than 1 engine in cluster rockets)
RDIAM	rocket diameter (in.)
*	stands for the operation of multiplication

TABLE 1.   Centuri Javelin

```
        CD=    .4
  RWT*RNE=    .6
    RDIAM=   .75
      RNE=    1
```

ENGINE (NAR)	MAX ALT (FT)	C.TIME (SEC)	MAX ACC (G'S)	AVG ACC (G'S)	EJ ALT (FT)	$/FT-ALT ($)
1/4A 3←1	60	1.8	20	7.8	60	$3.62-03
1/4A 3←2	59	1.8	20	7.6	59	$3.65-03
1/2A 6←2	219	3.5	41	19.3	219	$1.07-03
A 5←2	612	5.5	39	14.5	612	$4.36-04
A 8←3	645	5.7	41	23.8	645	$4.14-04
B 4←2	1413	7.1	37	10.8	1413	$2.12-04
B 4←4	1440	7.1	36	10.4	1440	$2.08-04
B 4←6	1437	7.1	35	10.1	1437	$2.09-04
B 6←4	1366	7.4	35	15.0	1366	$2.20-04
B 14←5	1428	7.6	87	41.1	1428	$2.33-04
C 6←3	2594	8.3	32	12.4	2594	$1.22-04
C 6←5	2639	8.4	32	12.2	2639	$1.20-04
1/4A 3←4	58	1.8	20	7.5	45	$3.73-03
1/2A 6←4	221	3.5	40	19.1	220	$1.05-03
A 5←4	609	5.4	37	13.9	609	$4.38-04
A 8←5	632	5.6	39	22.8	632	$4.22-04
B 6←6	1436	7.4	37	15.9	1436	$2.09-04
B 14←6	1430	7.6	86	40.5	1430	$2.33-04
B 14←7	1423	7.6	84	39.8	1423	$2.34-04
C 6←7	2651	8.5	31	12.0	2651	$1.19-04

TABLE 2.   Centuri Javelin

CD=   .7
RWT*RNE=   .6
RDIAM=   .75
RNE=   1

ENGINE (NAR)	MAX ALT (FT)	C.TIME (SEC)	MAX ACC (G'S)	AVG ACC (G'S)	EJ ALT (FT)	$/FT-ALT ($)
1/4A 3←1	57	1.8	20	7.7	57	$3.80-03
1/4A 3←2	58	1.7	20	7.6	57	$3.75-03
1/2A 6←2	197	3.3	41	19.2	197	$1.18-03
A 5←2	491	4.8	39	14.2	491	$5.43-04
A 8←3	522	4.9	41	23.5	522	$5.11-04
B 4←2	1030	5.8	37	10.0	1030	$2.91-04
B 4←4	1079	5.8	36	9.7	1079	$2.78-04
B 4←6	1082	5.8	35	9.5	1082	$2.77-04
B 6←4	1029	6.1	35	14.4	1029	$2.92-04
B 14←5	1050	6.2	87	40.1	1050	$3.17-04
C 6←3	1824	6.5	32	10.8	1824	$1.74-04
C 6←5	1873	6.5	32	10.7	1873	$1.69-04
1/4A 3←4	57	1.7	20	7.5	34	$3.82-03
1/2A 6←4	202	3.3	40	19.0	200	$1.16-03
A 5←4	508	4.8	37	13.6	508	$5.25-04
A 8←5	520	4.9	39	22.5	520	$5.12-04
B 6←6	1069	6.0	37	15.1	1069	$2.81-04
B 14←6	1053	6.2	86	39.5	1053	$3.17-04
B 14←7	1048	6.2	84	38.9	1045	$3.18-04
C 6←7	1880	6.6	31	10.5	1880	$1.68-04

TABLE 3.   Penetrator

```
        CD=    .6
       RWT=    variable
     RDIAM=    .9
       RNE=    1
```

ENGINE (NAR)		MAX ALT (FT)	C.TIME (SEC)	MAX ACC (G'S)	AVG ACC (G'S)	EJ ALT (FT)	$/FT-ALT ($)
A	4←4	216	3.2	24	5.0	214	$1.08-03
B	3←4	603	4.7	23	3.3	603	$4.42-04
B	3←6	605	4.7	23	3.3	600	$4.41-04
C	4←4	1258	6.2	29	3.9	1258	$2.39-04
C	4←6	1273	6.2	29	3.9	1273	$2.36-04
D	4←6	1567	6.6	21	3.8	1567	$3.83-04
D	4←8	1568	6.6	21	3.8	1561	$3.83-04
D	6←6	1932	7.3	35	6.8	1932	$3.28-04
D	6←8	1937	7.3	35	6.8	1936	$3.27-04
E	5←6	2878	7.6	29	3.4	2878	$3.18-04
F	7←6	6159	9.4	23	2.1	6159	$3.79-04

TABLE 4.   F.S.I. Voyager with 2-oz. Load

```
         CD=    .75
    RWT*RNE=    5.3
      RDIAM=    1.14
        RNE=    1
```

ENGINE (NAR)		MAX ALT (FT)	C.TIME (SEC)	MAX ACC (G'S)	AVG ACC (G'S)	EJ ALT (FT)	$/FT-ALT ($)
A	4←4	19	.8	9	1.1	0	$1.21-02
B	3←4	55	1.1	9	.6	38	$4.84-03
B	3←6	55	1.1	9	.6	8	$4.84-03
C	4←4	221	2.6	11	1.1	216	$1.36-03
C	4←6	221	2.6	11	1.1	196	$1.36-03
D	4←6	326	3.1	8	1.1	309	$1.84-03
D	4←8	326	3.1	8	1.1	278	$1.84-03
D	6←6	610	4.8	14	2.5	607	$1.04-03
D	6←8	610	4.8	14	2.5	588	$1.04-03
E	5←6	1044	5.3	13	1.4	1043	$8.78-04
F	7←6	3128	7.5	13	1.2	3128	$7.46-04

TABLE 5.   Astron Scrambler with 2-oz. Egg

                CD=   .75
               RWT=   1.6
             RDIAM=   1.8
               RNE=   3

ENGINE (NAR)	MAX ALT (FT)	C.TIME (SEC)	MAX ACC (G'S)	AVG ACC (G'S)	EJ ALT (FT)	$/FT-ALT ($)
1/4A 3←1	15	.8	11	3.5	15	$1.47-02
1/4A 3←2	14	.8	10	3.5	8	$1.51-02
1/2A 6←2	63	1.8	22	9.7	63	$3.72-03
A 5←2	196	3.1	21	7.3	196	$1.36-03
A 8←3	211	3.3	22	12.1	211	$1.26-03
B 4←2	508	4.5	21	5.4	508	$5.91-04
B 4←4	530	4.4	21	5.3	530	$5.66-04
B 4←6	522	4.4	20	5.2	510	$5.75-04
B 6←4	516	4.6	20	8.0	516	$5.82-04
B 14←5	542	4.9	49	21.8	542	$6.15-04
C 6←3	1065	5.6	19	6.5	1065	$2.97-04
C 6←5	1094	5.6	19	6.4	1094	$2.90-04
1/4A 3←4	14	.8	10	3.5	0	$1.52-02
1/2A 6←4	62	1.8	21	9.6	40	$3.76-03
A 5←4	196	3.1	21	7.1	191	$1.36-03
A 8←5	205	3.2	22	11.8	189	$1.30-03
B 6←6	532	4.6	21	8.2	523	$5.64-04
B 14←6	539	4.9	49	21.6	533	$6.19-04
B 14←7	535	4.9	48	21.4	514	$6.23-04
C 6←7	1089	5.6	19	6.3	1079	$2.91-04

TABLE 6.   Giant Load Lifter with 7-oz. Payload

	CD=	.8
RWT*RNE=	9.5	
RDIAM=	2	
RNE=	4	

ENGINE (NAR)	MAX ALT (FT)	C.TIME (SEC)	MAX ACC (G'S)	AVG ACC (G'S)	EJ ALT (FT)	$/FT-ALT ($)
A 4←4	99	2.1	17	3.1	87	$2.36-03
B 3←4	302	3.3	16	2.0	300	$8.84-04
B 3←6	302	3.3	16	2.0	278	$8.84-04
C 4←4	754	4.9	21	2.6	754	$3.98-04
C 4←6	757	4.9	21	2.6	753	$3.96-04
D 4←6	974	5.4	15	2.6	973	$6.16-04
D 4←8	974	5.4	15	2.6	951	$6.16-04
D 6←6	1297	6.3	25	4.8	1297	$4.88-04
D 6←8	1298	6.3	25	4.8	1288	$4.88-04
E 5←6	1990	6.6	22	2.5	1990	$4.61-04
F 7←6	4490	8.0	20	1.6	4490	$5.20-04
1/4A 3←1	7	.5	8	2.3	6	$3.09-02
1/4A 3←2	7	.5	8	2.3	0	$3.14-02
1/2A 6←2	34	1.3	16	6.8	32	$6.94-03
A 5←2	118	2.4	16	5.1	118	$2.25-03
A 8←3	127	2.6	16	8.7	127	$2.09-03
B 4←2	363	3.9	16	3.9	363	$8.27-04
B 4←4	368	3.9	15	3.8	368	$8.14-04
B 4←6	361	3.8	15	3.8	345	$8.31-04
B 6←4	369	4.1	15	5.9	369	$8.13-04
B 14←5	404	4.5	37	16.1	402	$8.26-04
C 6←3	918	5.7	15	5.2	918	$3.45-04
C 6←5	936	5.7	15	5.1	936	$3.38-04
1/4A 3←4	7	.5	8	2.3	0	$3.17-02
1/2A 6←4	33	1.3	16	6.8	9	$6.99-03
A 5←4	115	2.4	15	5.0	106	$2.32-03
A 8←5	123	2.5	16	8.5	103	$2.16-03
B 6←6	381	4.1	16	6.0	369	$7.87-04
B 14←6	401	4.4	36	16.0	392	$8.32-04
B 14←7	397	4.4	36	15.9	375	$8.39-04
C 6←7	929	5.7	14	5.1	923	$3.41-04

TABLE 7. Centuri Defender

CD=	.85
RWT*RNE=	2
RDIAM=	1.64
RNE=	3

ENGINE (NAR)	MAX ALT (FT)	C.TIME (SEC)	MAX ACC (G'S)	AVG ACC (G'S)	EJ ALT (FT)	$/FT-ALT $
1/4A 3←1	47	1.6	19	7.2	47	$4.57-03
1/4A 3←2	49	1.6	19	7.1	48	$4.42-03
1/2A 6←2	156	2.9	38	18.0	156	$1.50-03
A 5←2	349	3.9	37	13.0	349	$7.63-04
A 8←3	376	4.0	39	21.6	376	$7.09-04
B 4←2	688	4.4	35	8.4	688	$4.36-04
B 4←4	739	4.5	34	8.3	739	$4.06-04
B 4←6	735	4.5	33	8.1	717	$4.08-04
B 6←4	706	4.7	33	12.6	706	$4.25-04
B 14←5	698	4.8	82	36.4	698	$4.78-04
C 6←3	1208	4.9	31	8.5	1208	$2.62-04
C 6←5	1239	4.9	30	8.4	1239	$2.56-04
1/4A 3←4	48	1.6	19	7.0	2	$4.49-03
1/2A 6←4	160	2.8	38	17.8	149	$1.46-03
A 5←4	372	3.9	35	12.5	372	$7.17-04
A 8←5	376	4.0	37	20.8	368	$7.10-04
B 6←6	718	4.7	35	13.1	704	$4.18-04
B 14←6	697	4.8	81	35.9	685	$4.78-04
B 14←7	695	4.8	80	35.4	659	$4.79-04
C 6←7	1238	5.0	30	8.4	1206	$2.56-04

TABLE 8.   Astron Scout

CD=   1.4
RWT*RNE=   .28
RDIAM=   .765
RNE=   1

ENGINE (NAR)	MAX ALT (FT)	C.TIME (SEC)	MAX ACC (G'S)	AVG ACC (G'S)	EJ ALT (FT)	$/FT-ALT ($)
1/4A 3←1	77	2.2	29	11.3	77	$2.81-03
1/4A 3←2	93	2.1	28	11.0	93	$2.32-03
1/2A 6←2	210	3.1	57	26.7	210	$1.11-03
A 5←2	386	3.7	53	17.9	386	$6.91-04
A 8←3	414	3.7	56	30.5	414	$6.44-04
B 4←2	693	3.8	49	9.8	693	$4.33-04
B 4←4	742	3.8	47	9.7	742	$4.04-04
B 4←6	742	3.9	45	9.5	688	$4.04-04
B 6←4	707	4.1	45	15.4	707	$4.24-04
B 14←5	663	4.1	115	47.7	652	$5.03-04
C 6←3	1164	4.0	41	8.8	1164	$2.72-04
C 6←5	1180	4.0	40	8.8	1168	$2.68-04
1/4A 3←4	92	2.1	28	10.8	48	$2.36-03
1/2A 6←4	226	3.1	56	26.4	217	$1.03-03
A 5←4	423	3.7	50	17.1	422	$6.31-04
A 8←5	419	3.8	53	29.0	400	$6.37-04
B 6←6	706	4.0	49	15.9	657	$4.25-04
B 14←6	665	4.1	113	47.1	621	$5.02-04
B 14←7	667	4.2	111	46.3	576	$5.00-04
C 6←7	1183	4.1	39	8.8	1090	$2.68-04

Appendix 4   Metric Systems and Equivalents

Metric System and Equivalents

Basic Prefixes and Units

Prefixes		Meaning	Fraction	Decimal
MICRO-	=	one millionth	$\frac{1}{1,000,000}$	.000001
MILLI-	=	one thousandth	$\frac{1}{1000}$	.001
CENT-	=	one hundredth	$\frac{1}{100}$	.01
DECI-	=	one tenth	$\frac{1}{10}$	.1
UNIT	=	one	1	1.
DEKA-	=	ten	$\frac{10}{1}$	10.
HECTO-	=	one hundred	$\frac{100}{1}$	100.
KILO-	=	one thousand	$\frac{1000}{1}$	1000.
MYRIA-	=	ten thousand	$\frac{10,000}{1}$	10,000.
MEGA	=	one million	$\frac{1,000,000}{1}$	1,000,000.

Base Units

"METER" for length
"GRAM" for weight or mass
"LITER" for capacity

Force

4.45 NEWTONS = 1 pound
.222 POUNDS = 1 newton

Common U.S.A. Equivalents

Length			
	1 inch	=	25.4001 millimeters
	1 millimeter	=	0.03937 inch
	1 foot	=	0.304801 meter
	1 meter	=	3.28083 feet
	1 yard	=	0.914402 meter
	1 meter	=	1.093611 yards
	1 mile	=	1.609347 kilometers
	1 kilometer	=	0.621370 mile

Capacity (Liquid)

1 quart	=	0.94633 liter
1 liter	=	1.05671 quarts
1 gallon	=	3.78533 liters
1 liter	=	0.26418 gallon

Capacity (Dry)

1 quart	=	1.012 liters
1 liter	=	0.9081 quart
1 peck	=	8.810 liters
1 liter	=	0.11351 peck

Mass (Avoirdupois)

1 ounce	=	28.350 grams
1 gram	=	0.035274 ounce
1 pound	=	0.45359 kilogram
1 kilogram	=	2.20462 pounds

Glossary

ACCELERATION A change in the velocity of an object. If an object goes from 200 mph to 400 mph, this is *positive acceleration;* if from 400 mph to 200 mph, it is *negative acceleration.*

ACCELEROMETER A device that measures acceleration, usually in Gs.

AIRFOIL Any surface such as a fin or wing designed to aid in lifting, controlling, or stabilizing a bird. Model rocket fins should be designed for controlling and stabilizing only.

AMATEUR ROCKETRY Unlike model rocketry, *amateur rocketry* involves the compounding of explosives by the user and the making of rockets out of metal. When supervised by men trained in the handling of explosives and in internal ballistics, it is relatively safe, but it is serious business rather than a hobby. Bunkers and large tracts of land are essential.

BALSA A lightweight wood used in building model rockets and airplanes.

BASEMENT BOMBER Someone who compounds his own propellants, either through ignorance or a subconscious suicide wish. He has a one-in-seven chance of being killed or maimed for each year he continues to experiment.

BLAST DEFLECTOR A strip of metal on the launch pad that directs the exhaust of the model rocket away from the fins and the combustible wooden base.

BODY TUBE A paper, plastic, or balsa tube; the main part of a model rocket.

BOOSTER One of the stages in a multistage model rocket, consisting of a section of body tube, engine mount, and fins.

BOOST-GLIDER or B/G A model rocket designed to be launched vertically and glide back to earth.

BURNOUT The point at which an engine ceases to produce significant thrust, even if the ejection charge and smoke delay are still intact.

CLUSTER ROCKET A rocket in which two or more engines are fired simultaneously.

DELAY The time between burnout and ejection in a rocket. Usually smoke is created during the delay for tracking purposes.

DOPE A nitrate- or butyrate-based lacquer used on balsa and paper but not on most plastics.

DURATION The time from the beginning of something until the end. Duration of thrust, for example, would be the time from ignition to burnout.

EJECTION Expelling an object from a container. For example, a parachute is *ejected* from a body tube.

EJECTION CHARGE A small explosive charge in a model rocket engine that deploys the recovery device. Booster engines do not have an ejection charge.

ELECTRIC MATCH A highly sensitive ignition element requiring only a slight amount of electricity to be set off. Electric match is usually used only in large clusters and D- through F-class engines.

ENGINE, BOOSTER An engine specifically designed to ignite another engine on burnout. No delay or ejection charge is built in.

ENGINES, LIQUID-FUEL MODEL ROCKET Lightweight aluminum construction powered by pressurized non-combustible gas. At present this fuel is difluorodichloromethane.

ENGINE, MODEL ROCKET Non-metallic engines produced commercially under controlled conditions specifically for use in model rockets.

FINS Thin pieces of balsa attached to the body tube that guide the model rocket in flight like feathers on an arrow.

FUEL The substance burned to produce thrust in a model rocket engine.

GRAIN The direction of the fibers in balsa. If a sheet of balsa is bent along the line of grain, it will break very easily.

G The measure of stress acceleration puts on an object. The earth's gravity puts a stress of one G on every object.

IGNITER An electrical element that creates enough heat to fire a model rocket engine.

IGNITION The point at which the propellant in a model rocket engine catches fire.

JET PROPULSION The forward propulsion of a rocket by the rearward discharge of a high-speed stream of hot gases produced by the combination of the rocket fuel and oxidizer.

LAUNCH The lift-off of a rocket after ignition.

LAUNCH LUG Small pieces of balsa, paper, or plastic that enable the rocket to be guided in initial flight by either a launch rod or rail.

LAUNCH RAIL A hollow metal tube with a slot down one side. The launch lug (in the form of a small T of balsa or a nylon screw) slips inside the rail.

LAUNCH ROD A piece of metal wire ($\frac{1}{8}$- to $\frac{1}{4}$-inch thick). In this case, launch lug is usually a soda straw that slips over the rod.

LAUNCH TOWER   Usually a construction in which the rocket fins fit in slots to guide the rocket in its initial phase of flight.

LEAD WIRE   The wire between the launch panel and the micro-clips and igniter. Lamp cord is used for this in most model rocket launching systems.

METRIC SYSTEM   A system of weights and measures based on decimals. This makes conversion from one unit to the next a simple matter of moving decimal points.

MICRO-CLIPS   Small alligator clips that attach the lead wires to the igniter.

MODEL ROCKET   Listen, man, read the book!

MULTISTAGE ROCKET   A rocket with two or more stages.

MYLAR   A super-strong lightweight plastic used in body tubes for ultra-high-altitude model rockets.

NEWTON   A metric unit of force. 4.45 newtons of thrust is equal to 1 pound of thrust. Abbreviation: N.

NEWTON-SECONDS   The metric unit of total impulse.

NICHROME WIRE   A wire that glows red hot when electricity is passed through it. Nichrome is the standard element in most igniters.

NOSE CONE   The front portion of a model rocket made from balsa, paper, or plastic. The nose cone serves to form the aerodynamic shape of the model so it passes easily through the air with the least drag.

NOZZLE   The part of a model rocket engine (usually ceramic) that directs the flow of exhaust gases.

OXIDIZER   A substance that, when burned, gives off a gas that supports combustion. Part of a rocket's propellant must be oxidizer.

PARACHUTE   A folding, umbrella-like contrivance made of plastic, silk, nylon, or tough rice paper used to slow the descent of a model rocket.

POUND   The English measure of thrust. One pound is equal to 4.45 newtons.

POUND-SECONDS   The English unit of total impulse.

PROPELLANT   A combination of oxidizer and fuel that burns in a model rocket engine and produces thrust without an outside air supply.

SAFETY SWITCH   An extra switch on a launch pad that is kept in the "OFF" position until the final 10 seconds of countdown. It is used to prevent the accidental launching of a model rocket.

SEPARATOR   A device used to deploy the recovery system in a liquid-fuel model rocket.

STREAMER   A strip of crepe paper or colored plastic used in small model rockets as part of the recovery device.

SUPERSONIC SPEED   The speed at which a model rocket breaks the sound barrier. At this point the compressibility of the air changes and shock waves are set up resulting in a small "boom."

THRUST   The force (in pounds or newtons) that a model rocket engine exerts.

THRUST-TIME CURVE OR THRUST-TIME PERFORMANCE GRAPH   A graph of the performance of an engine showing the high and low points of thrust at various time intervals.

T-MAX   The time it takes from ignition to the point of maximum thrust.

TOTAL IMPULSE   The average thrust of a model rocket engine multiplied by the duration. Under theoretical drag-free conditions, two times the total impulse would send the rocket to twice the altitude.

VELOCITY   The speed in a given direction.

VERNIER ROCKETS   Small rockets used in guiding space vehicles. They do not produce an appreciable amount of thrust, only enough to steer the craft.

WEIGHT   The force exerted by acceleration on a certain mass. For example, the acceleration of one G (the earth's gravity) exerted on a 1-kilogram object would weigh 2.2 pounds in English units.

WIND TUNNEL   A large box through which air flows at a given velocity. A wind tunnel is used to test rocket stability and aerodynamic forces.

INDEX

(Page numbers in italics refer to photographs and diagrams)

Library, use of. *See* Reference books and material, model rocketry
Liquid-fuel model rockets, 6, *20*, 24, 25, 26–27, 36; parachute recovery of, 56
Logarithms, natural, 130–32

Malewicki, Douglas J., method of estimating effects of drag on altitude calculations by, 47–51
Mandell, Gordon, "Aerodynamic Force Effects on Model Rocket Motion" by, 121
Masking tape, use of, 9, 10
Match-head rockets, 1
Materials and supplies. *See* Tools and supplies; specific kinds
Maximum thrust, defined, 21
Metric system of weights and measures and equivalents, use of, 16, *20*, 143–44
Micro-clips, use of, *31*, 39, 40, 66
M.I.T. Model Rocket Society, 121
Model rocketry (*see also* Model rockets): defined, 1–4; history, 4–6; safety, 1–2, 3, 4, 22–24; tools and supplies, 9–12
Model rockets, *ii, 3, 11, 15, 31, 60, 78, 80* (*see also* Model rocketry); basic parts and construction, 12–17; liquid-fuel, *20, 25;* payload, *64, 90*
Moon, David, *31;* computer performance charts by, 51, 135–42
Multi-stage rockets, 59–67; launching, 63; second stage, *61;* two-stage, 59, *60*

National Association of Rocketry (NAR), *5,* 79, 96, 117; competitions and meets, 79, 113, 117; engine classification system, 25; National Meet Research and Development contest, 113; regulations, 29, 83
Newton, Sir Isaac, his Third Law of Motion, 19
Newtons, measurement of thrust and, *20*, 21, 147
Nichrome wire igniter, 29, 35, 36, 147

Nose-blow recovery, 15, 54, 57
Nose cones, *11*, 12–13, 91
Notebooks, use of, 9, 10, 109

Organizations, model rocket, 127–28
Oxidizers, *20*, 147

Paint, use of, 9, 10–11
Paintbrushes, use of, 9, 10
Parachute recovery, 11, *15*, 54–56, 55, 57
Payload capsule, 70, 71, 74
Payload rocket models, 69–75; accelerometer, *74,* 74–75; camera, 71–72, *72;* egg, *64,* 71; engines for, 70–71; kinds, 71–75; large-scale, 89, *90;* live, 69; radio transmitters, *74;* recovery systems for, 70, 71
Performance tabulations, model rocket, tables of, 135–42
Port-burner (core-burner) engines, 26
Power pod, B/G, 87, *87*
Pressure. *See* Center of Gravity and Pressure (CG and CP)
Projects, model rocket. *See* Science fair displays and projects
Propellants, 19–20, 24, 25, 26–28. *See also* Liquid-fuel model rockets; Solid-fuel model rockets
Protractors, use in tracking, 96–97, 101
Publications, model rocket, listed, 127

Radio transmitters, model rocket payload, 73–74
Rail, launch. *See* Launch rail
Reading material. *See* Reference books and material, model rocketry
Recovery (recovery systems), 2, *11,* 12, 15, 27, 53–57, 67; basic principles, 56–57; boost-gliders and, 56, 57, 77, 78, 79; heavy-duty, 57; for large-scale model rockets, 93–94; payload capsules, 70, 71
Reference books and material, model rocketry, 108, *108,* 111–12, 118; alphabetical listing of, 123–26, 127